more paperwork

more paperwork

**exploring the potential of paper
in design and architecture**

written and designed by
nancy williams

Phaidon Press Limited
Regent's Wharf
All Saints Street
London N1 9PA

Phaidon Press Inc.
180 Varick Street
New York, NY 10014

www.phaidon.com

First published 2005
© 2005 Phaidon Press Limited

ISBN 0 7148 4364 4

A CIP catalogue record for this book
is available from the British Library.

Printed in China

more paperwork contents

author's notes
The cover and many of the
chapter dividers have been
prepared for you to complete
by hand.
Throughout the book you will
see this square ■ It indicates a
project that involves some form
of recycling, whether it uses
a recycled stock or item,
or is made from the remnants
of another product.

7 introduction

11 two dimensional

13 **surface qualities and effects**

33 **cutting and folding**

53 **binding**

69 **interactive**

81 **mixed media**

93 three dimensional

97 **architecture**

109 **exhibition and sculpture**

121 **fashion and accessories**

133 **packaging**

145 **product**

161 terms and techniques

173 index

Paper is amazing. You can write, draw, paint and print on it, you can cut and fold it, you can mould it, and that's not all – the list of things you can do with it is boundless. It's not only designers that appreciate the characteristics of paper and see its importance. In a recent survey, in which leading mathematicians and scientists were asked what they believed to be the most significant inventions of the last two millennia, the invention of paper was cited for the role it has played in 'breaking down barriers of time and distance and permitting unprecedented growth and opportunity'.

history The story of paper is intriguing. You might justifiably presume that the spread of papermaking techniques throughout the world would have been swift, but it took more than 1,000 years for these skills to travel from the East to the West. It is also surprising that, with such a simple technology, the gestation period between the introduction of paper and learning how to make it was usually between two and three hundred years.

In the West, we generally consider paper to be an ordinary disposable commodity, albeit a vital one. By contrast, in the East, paper was once one of the most precious and valued materials. It was created in China around the end of the first century for the court of Emperor Ho Ti by Ts'ai Lun. As chamberlain, he was responsible for the Imperial library and was determined to find a better form of recording information than the bamboo and silk that were used at the time. He worked with craftsmen over many years, developing existing techniques previously used for making cloth and wrappings. Experimenting with many different materials, he found the bark of the mulberry tree provided the best source of paper fibre. It produced a smooth and flexible sheet – the forerunner of writing paper today.

Five hundred years later, paper was introduced to Japan by a Korean Buddhist priest, in the form of sacred texts. Once they obtained the knowledge of basic papermaking skills, the Japanese worked hard to find ways of further improving the quality of the surface, taking it to new levels of sophistication.

8   The paper produced was originally used for religious documents but soon became extremely sought after and came to represent financial, intellectual and spiritual wealth. Through association, paper itself became venerated, as did the papermaking process, which was seen very much as an art – rather like the teamaking ceremony. This deep respect for paper could explain why the Japanese have been able to push the boundaries of what paper can be used for, further than any other nation. They believe in it and are prepared to invest in it. Like the Inuits with their myriad of words for snow, the Japanese have an abundance of terms for different types of paper, their properties and uses (see terms and techniques).

Due to the strength provided by the extremely long grain of Japanese paper – 2 to 15mm long compared with less than 2mm in the West – they have a long tradition of using paper for items such as clothing, dining utensils, interior decorations and toys. Paper became so important to the economy that the export of paper goods was second only to that of rice. Not surprising, then, the prominence of the Japanese when it comes to all things paper.

During the eighth century papermaking techniques spread from Japan across Central Asia to Baghdad and then on to Damascus, but it wasn't until the eleventh century that they reached Spain. Even then, the progress of papermaking across the rest of Europe took another unbelievable five hundred years and didn't reach Russia or the United States until the end of the seventeenth century.

resurgence of paper Whereas the demise of paper products was widely anticipated due to the advent of the personal computer, precisely the opposite appears to have happened – people are using paper more than ever. Paper production continues to rise every year – hopefully, not entirely due to the sea of mailers that come through the post and which are stuffed into magazines.

Designers from all disciplines have rediscovered paper and, in reassessing its possibilities, which by-and-large have been taken for granted, are finding that it is capable of ever more extraordinary things.

Paper companies are also pushing the boundaries, creating new products to feed the ever hungry market. It is now possible to obtain off-the-shelf papers that are heat sensitive, have inclusions of all descriptions and are technically very advanced. There are papers with rubberized surfaces, papers treated to improve their foldability, papers that are tear resistant – even papers that are washable. Pearlized, metalicized and other types of translucent paper are also available. You can buy preprinted papers, flocked papers, veneered papers and embroidered papers. The choice is seemingly endless.

As well as the papers intended for designers, craftspeople and artists, there is a diversity of papers produced to fulfil specific jobs, including filter paper, lens tissue and sandpaper. These can broaden the spectrum of opportunities open to the designer even further.

handmade paper Not only in Japan, but all over the world, making paper by hand is once again being treated as an art form. Following a resurgence of the craft in America during the Sixties, craftspeople are keen to spread the word. Papermaking is now being taught in colleges and schools. You can buy papermaking kits and books from craft shops and through the Internet. There are even regular journals on the subject.

The range of ethnic handmade papers presently available is impressive, as can be seen by looking at the origins of papers obtainable from fine paper merchants – China, Egypt, India, Korea, Mexico, Nepal, Philippines and Thailand. Many of these countries, China being the obvious example, have had a long tradition of papermaking, but it is only in recent years that they have started re-exporting, due to the demands of the West.

It took papermaking techniques a long time to travel the world, but, due to the modest set-up costs of this industry, it has become increasingly popular in many developing countries. Aid organizations are working with communities to set up papermaking for their own use and to help them develop their economies.

recycling In the West we think of recycling as a new concept, whereas in most of the rest of the world it has been the practice from the beginning. Once again, in cultures in which paper was considered valuable, it was natural for every possible scrap to be recycled. Special terms were coined for these papers as long ago as 800 AD.

Finally in the West we are beginning to fully embrace the concept of recycling, though even ten years ago some paper manufacturers seemed to be resisting the pressure to produce truly recycled paper. Similarly, many designers and clients alike were reluctant to use recycled stock, due to the perceived compromise in reproduction quality. Now everyone is keen to be seen to support the environment. And, due to improved production techniques, the quality of recycled paper offers a printing surface that is often hard to differentiate from virgin paper. At the same time, designers have learnt to appreciate the qualities of an overtly recycled piece of paper, enjoying its honesty and appearance.

When recycled paper was first produced in the West, there was a raging debate as to its overall efficacy, though it is now widely accepted that recycling has both economical and environmental benefits. Many paper companies now take this aspect of paper production so seriously that they produce comprehensive environmental policy documents, in which every aspect of the production process is looked at in terms of energy efficiency and effects on the environment. The aim is to create the least impact on the environment and many companies are rightly proud of their efforts. There are affiliations that go as far as producing 'Paper Profiles', which provide key information regarding every aspect of a paper and its production process, including composition, environmental parameters and management, even wood procurement, in order that the caring consumer can make an appropriate and informed choice.

The paper industry is now one of the world's largest recyclers. In Britain it is the largest, with an increase in volume of more than eighty per cent in the last ten years – recycling of paper is now more than three times that of glass and nine times that of plastic. Recycled materials now represent sixty-six per cent of original production, and that is with the involvement of only two thirds of paper companies. In many European countries the figures are even better, with Austria recycling close to a hundred per cent of the paper it collects and Sweden not far behind.

The actual source of the recycling product was once rather anonymous, so you might only have been told that it was made from rag or post-consumer waste. Now paper companies are proud to tell you. There is even a range of papers made from recycled beer labels named after different types of beer. In addition, there are many products made from recycled cartons, in which clues to their former existence are clearly evident.

Recycling isn't only to do with forming new, pristine sheets of paper and board from old. It is often about taking a redundant or discarded product and transforming it into something else – for example, a poster into a waste bin. Sometimes it is about using every piece of the paper or board, so that the waste from one object is transformed into another – a book from badge offcuts or a pencil rest from a coat hanger. There is something extremely satisfying about this approach and it is encouraging to see how many designers, across the disciplines, have this principle at the core of their work ethic.

summary When you think about it, paper contributes to almost all aspects of our everyday lives, at work and at play, from the mundane toilet roll or tissue or the daily paper we read to the stationery in our supposed paper-less office, the wrapping of our purchases and, of course, the money we use to pay for all these things. The evidence indicates that paper is very much here to stay and in ever more infinite guises. It is clear that it is such an integral part of our lives and of all our cultures that, I believe, it would be impossible for us to ever stop exploiting and developing paper. We enjoy it too much to abandon it – the way it looks, its tactile qualities, even the way it sounds and the precious, as well as not so precious, things we make from it.

I have certainly enjoyed the privilege of seeing the work that has been reproduced in this book, as well as the work that there was not enough space for, and I hope that you will find the following pages both interesting and stimulating. I look forward to the next ten years and to the inventive and inspirational ideas that designers and architects will employ in their use of paper.

more paperwork is divided into two sections. The two-dimensional section covers graphic design, while the three-dimensional section covers architecture, fashion, exhibition and sculpture, packaging and product, some of which contain three-dimensional aspects of graphic design. The section in which an item appears is, in some instances, arbitrary. Mostly the works are categorized by their predominant feature.

As with **paperwork**, this book also provides the opportunity for the reader to partake in creating a variety of forms and objects in the chapter openers.chapter openers.

A decade ago, the end of paper-based design was being heralded alongside the advent of the PC. Graphic designers were concerned that their skills might become redundant, with clients generating their own communications. Many designers started to develop their technological skills instead, concentrating on interactive solutions for their clients. However, once the initial threat of this new medium died down and everyone became comfortable with it and realized its limitations, there was space and opportunities for both media. Ironically, paper is now valued more than ever, and designers are playing and experimenting with it in a way that only a minority did previously – a trend possibly reflected in the thirty per cent increase in paper consumption over the last ten years.

The preoccupation of many graphic designers, including myself, with creating a pristine object is being eroded. Much of the design work produced today is more akin to fine art than traditional graphics, being, in many cases, the outcome of self-initiated projects rather than the result of a client brief. This is interesting, as graphic design has generally been viewed as the poor relation of fine art. Increasingly, designers are becoming interested in what they can do with paper, exploring old techniques and developing new ones to create works of beauty and self expression. As fashion trends become more diverse and more personalized, graphic design has followed suit and loosened up, providing solutions that are often quirky, amusing and idiosyncratic. This is evident in the diverse range of design styles that a single design practice can produce – from a high production, super glossy, pared-down brochure to a rustic piece, letterpressed onto unbleached, recycled paper. I believe that this comes from a confidence that designers have as much right to express themselves as anyone else and paper is their medium of choice.

It is also good to see that designers are still prepared to stand their ground when it comes to production values. Many of the more unusual printing and finishing techniques are certainly not cheap and their exponents are seldom easy to track down. Only if we carry on specifying these techniques do they have a chance of surviving.

12 **surface qualities and effects** As I have mentioned, the range of papers available to the graphic designer is as broad as ever, despite the fact that some of the smaller producers may have disappeared. The work represented in this section shows how the appropriate choice of paper can make all the difference and how, in some cases, it is all you need, along with simple typography, to achieve the required effect. The examples also demonstrate how the inherent qualities and properties of a paper can be exploited to create interest and drama. It also looks at how new and traditional techniques can be utilized to produce subtle and innovative results. What's more, the designer's standard kit of surface effects is now being augmented to include tearing, crumpling and even burning – whatever achieves the desired effect. There are no longer any confines.

cutting and folding While cutting and folding are the most basic finishing techniques available to the designer, it is amazing what can be achieved with a bit of ingenuity and imagination. Even one die-cut hole, adroitly placed, can provide emphasis or intrigue, and a whole series of them can be stunning. With the advent of laser cutting, the fineness and intricacy of the imagery cut into paper can be breathtaking. With folding, the simple introduction of asymmetry, whether in length or angle, can lead to fascinating effects. Folding can also magically transform an ordinary, flat sheet of paper into a three-dimensional object or structure, the epitome of this being origami. The combination of cutting and folding can open up endless possibilities, culminating in the pop-up.

Most of the work here demonstrates what can be achieved when a designer looks beyond the expected. One of the most ingenious projects in this section uses extremely simple die-cuts on consecutive pages which then interlock to bind the pages together. Another uses simple cutting and folding techniques to produce an exquisite model contained in its own box.

binding When it comes to binding techniques, graphic designers have, by and large, stuck to perfect binding. However, there are many more techniques that can be used, from the simplest folding together of two pieces of paper to full-blown bookbinding. There is, of course, a host of binding options in between – stapling or wire stitching, stab stitching, spiral or wiro, rubber bands, rivets, plastic or metal interscrews, sewing and wrapping.

As with folding, when it comes to binding, asymmetry can transport a document or book from the regular to the extraordinary. Likewise, page sizes need not be uniform: different stocks can be used. When folding is combined with binding, another ocean of options opens up. There are not just gate folds, but throw outs, throw ups and throw downs, concertina folds and French folds, which are becoming increasingly popular. And why bind just one book, when you can bind two, three or more inter-related books together?

This is one of the larger chapters in the book and the work is amongst the most inventive. It is as if designers have a hankering to practise the skills of the book binder. Whilst these were previously the preserve of the bookbinding professionals and a few specialized graphic designers, now it seems that many are keen to be involved in this craft. Though some of the most impressive examples utilize intricate bookbinding, a significant number use the simplest techniques but, in these cases, it is the added new twist that creates fresh and innovative work.

interactive Whilst this term is most commonly used in connection with computer programs, there is a long tradition of graphic designers that intentionally produce designs with which the recipient or owner can engage. What could be more enjoyable than playing a part in the evolution of a piece? It's exciting, no one knows exactly what the outcome may be – the results are as many and varied as the people participating. Many of the approaches here derive from children's games or toys, while others are more functional – whichever, the undeniable aim is to have fun.

mixed media It is often very difficult to decide in which section to place a piece of work, but there is usually an overriding factor that determines the appropriate place. However, sometimes the balance of elements defies categorization and it is those projects that are included here, along with projects that involve materials other than paper.

Designers are becoming braver and more adventurous when it comes to specifying non-paper materials. Many of these projects have a strong element of humour or wit, possibly engendered by the freedom of using a novel medium. However, they are generally combined with paper, the substance that still offers the best surface for communications of all descriptions.

more paperwork surface qualities and effects

It is often the simplest of things that have the greatest impact. Here the use of very basic sugar paper, in conjunction with the extremely thin format, helps to accentuate and build the drama of this one-liner story, a promotional piece for a copywriter ■

country
UK
design practice
hat-trick design
designers
Gareth Howat
Jim Sutherland
art directors
Gareth Howat
David Kimpton
Jim Sutherland
client
Scott Perry
printer/finisher
Gavin Martin Associates
stock
Paperback

The quality and honesty of the humble egg box makes it the perfect promotional piece for the launch of a book on packaging design. Off-the-shelf egg boxes were silkscreen printed with the invitation, which was sent out packed in feathers ■

country
UK
design practice
Lippa Pearce Design
designer
Harry Pearce
client
Lippa Pearce Design
printer/finisher
68 Frank
stock
pre-manufactured egg box

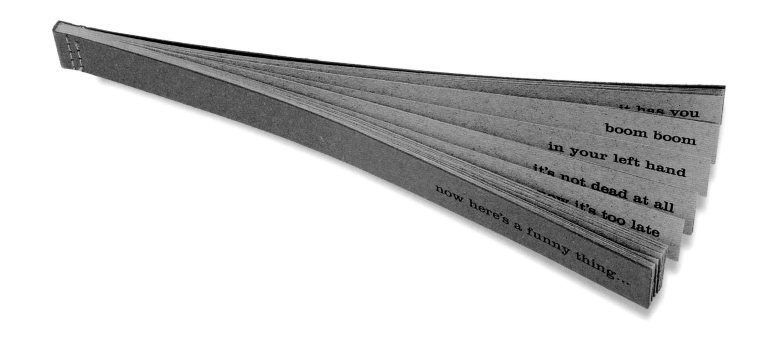

16 For most Mennonites, the
Bible is the only book they will
ever read. This was the
inspiration for the designers
of this elegant and serene book
of photographs, recording
photographer Larry Towell's
time with them. In order to
differentiate the experience of
reading and looking, a thin bible
paper was used for the text
and a coated art stock was
chosen for the pictures.
In addition, the bible paper is
cut short to fit the photographic
grid rather than the page grid.
The Bible influence is
emphasized by the plain black
cloth cover, slip case and
reading ribbon.

country
UK
design practice
Atelier Works
designers
Quentin Newark
David Hawkins
photographer
Larry Towell
client
Phaidon Press
stock
bible paper
matt-coated art

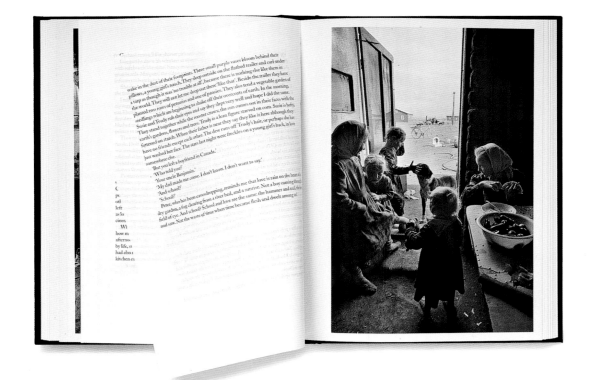

For this invitation to his 'garden wedding', the designer used bible paper. Exquisitely folded to secrete the text, it appeared, on removal from the slip case, to be covered in nothing but flowers. While being appropriate for the occasion, the delicate but strong nature of the paper is echoed in the delicate image of a flower meadow that flooded the paper.

country
UK
design practice
Cartlidge Levene
designer
Ian Cartlidge
client
Ian & Jo Cartlidge
printer/finisher
CTD Printers
stock
**Offenbach bible
paper 40gsm**

18   In this series of greetings
      cards the designer uses the
      transparency of the glassine
      window of the envelope
      to interact with the card inside.
      For example, the flames of
      the candles on a birthday cake
      light the candles of a
      candlestick, printed on the
      inside of the envelope, when
      the card is removed.

      country
      Japan
      design practice
      Draft
      designer
      Yoshie Watanabe
      client
      D-BROS
      printer/finisher
      Taiyo Printing Company
      stock
      Moderatone 128gsm
      Take-bulky 256gsm

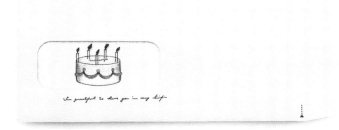

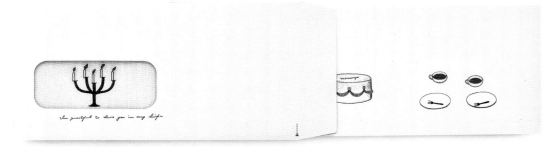

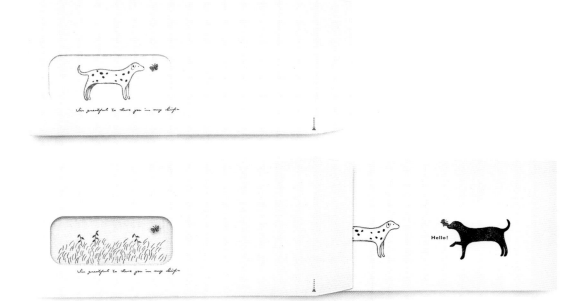

The use of a combination of opaque and transparent stocks in this identity achieves a multi-layered look for a high-tech company specializing in developing next generation software. The letterheads and die-cut business cards use the opacity of the paper to advantage, carrying a variety of colour images on the reverse – once you go to the expense of full-colour printing, the extra cost involved in multiple images is negligible. The transparency of the preprinted envelopes adds to the drama by allowing a tantalizing glimpse of the colourful letter inside.

country
Canada
design practice
Iridium
designer/art director
Mario L'Écuyer
client
Nexware Corporation
printer/finisher
Beauregard Printers
die-cutter
BLM Trade Printers
manufacturer
envelopes: Enveloppe Laurentide
stock
Gilbert Esse Texture White
Gilbert Gilclear Oxford

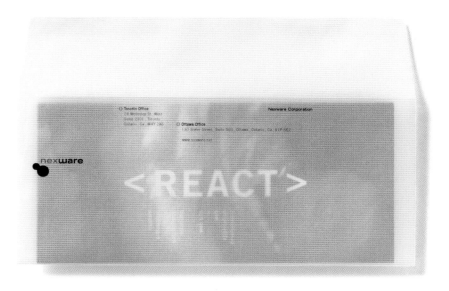

20 This wedding invitation uses a quality of paper that is generally avoided – its ability to be torn. Here it is used to brilliant effect. On receipt, it is necessary to tear the invitation apart to read the text inside, representing the inseparability of the couple.

country
Singapore
design practice
Kinetic Singapore
designers
Pann Lim
Roy Poh
art directors
Pann Lim
Andrew Lok
client
Lin Lim
Andrew Lok
printer/finisher
Shotech Press
stock
art card 300gsm

A WEDDING
INVITATION

IT'S HARD
TO TEAR
US APART.
So we decided to get married.
And we'd like you to be there.
It's at 6pm (the ceremony
starts at 7pm), on the 25th of May
at Tanjong Beach on Sentosa.
Kindly email us at
tanjongbeach@yahoo.com
to confirm your attendance.
Thank you.
Lin Lim & Andrew Lok

This annual report uses a series of torn photographs that have been repaired with tape, effectively printed in UV varnish, as a vivid metaphor for the work of this charity in helping people to piece their lives back together. All 9,000 covers were hand torn.

country
UK
design practice
hat-trick design
designers/art directors
Gareth Howat
David Kimpton
Jim Sutherland
client
Fairbridge
printer/finisher
Boss Print
stock
Command matt 180gsm, 350gsm

22

This American photography annual uses a technique that is, sadly, rarely used today. What appears to be an abstract pattern on the edge of the pages turns out to be a landscape when the pages are splayed. As you can just about see, this is achieved by printing, around the edge of each page, a progression of thin slices taken from the image.

country
USA
design practice
Sagmeister Inc
designers
Hjalti Karlsson
Stefan Sagmeister
art director
Stefan Sagmeister
client
Amilus
stock
matt-coated art 100gsm

A diary was the obvious vehicle for promoting a new twelve-colour printing press. At its heart are twelve pages of pure graphic pattern, which use each of the twelve units to print a special flat colour. Die-cut holes allow other patterns to be seen. The cover is blind debossed with a graphic representation of the months of the year, as shown in the detail below.

country
UK
design practice
williams and phoa
designers
Clifford Hiscock
Anthony Coyne
Valerie Kiock
Justin Davies
client
Taylor Bloxham
printer/finisher
Taylor Bloxham
stock
Premier Essential Gloss
Premier Essential Offset
Skivertex Vicuana 5232

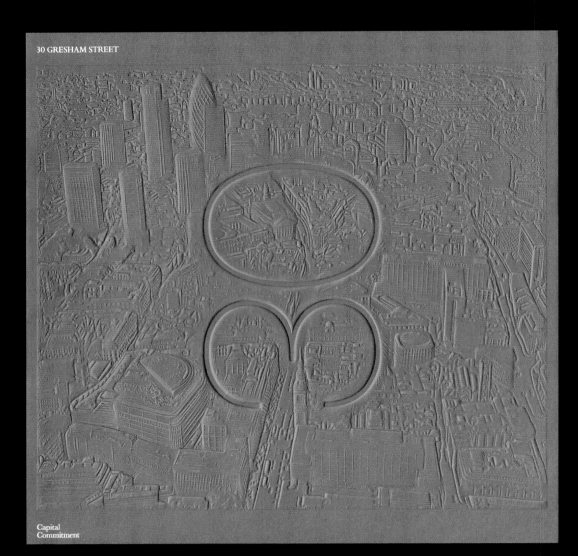

30 GRESHAM STREET

Capital
Commitment

The cover of this brochure, for a major property developer, uses an aerial photograph of the City of London that has been sculpturally embossed so that it appears to be emerging from the cover.

country
UK
design practice
hat-trick design
designers/art directors
Gareth Howat
David Kimpton
Jim Sutherland
client
Land Securities
printer/finisher
Gavin Martin Associates
stock
Colorplan 350gsm

This wonderfully subtle stationery for an interior designer practice uses the dramatic contrast of high-gloss and matt surfaces. The type of the letterhead is matt foil blocked in white onto a high-gloss label stock, while the type of the business cards combines blind debossing and a matt varnish.

country
UK
design practice
MadeThought
designers
Ben Parker
Paul Austin
client
Jump
printer/finisher
R Young & Son
stock
letterhead: Astralux
Label 115gsm
business cards:
Chromalux 300gsm

To celebrate D&AD's fortieth birthday a glamourous party theme was developed, based on the graphic style of the Forties. The covers of this invitation and commemorative book use Dufex, a process rarely seen outside the world of shimmering Christmas cards. It uses a specially formulated foil laminate in conjunction with an engraved embossing plate, to create this dazzling effect.

country
UK
design practice
NB: Studio
designer
Nick Vincent
art directors
Nick Finney
Ben Stott
Alan Dye
client
D&AD 'Forty'
printer/finisher
FJ Warren
stock
Dufex

The fifth in the Mohawk Paper's journal series 'Rethinking Design', this edition focused on how subcultures can inform design. Taking the form of a standard paperback book, it contrasts the lurid metallic, foil-blocked and embossed graphics – the vernacular of pulp fiction – with the smooth, velvety surface of the paper.

27

country
USA
design practice
Pentagram, New York
designers
Michael Bierut
Jacqueline Thaw
art director
Michael Bierut
client
Mohawk Paper Mills
printer/finisher
George Rice & Sons
stock
Mohawk Superfine

28 Made from intensely bright, fluorescent pink paper, the pages of this handmade book have been repeatedly screwed up then flattened, crumpled then smoothed out, scrunched up then pressed. As you turn the pages of the book, the harsh fluorescent paper becomes progressively creased, worn and degraded. Gradually, it is softer and more flexible, taking on the characteristics of fabric rather than paper. This is, in fact, very similar to a Japanese process that turns laminated paper into material for clothing.

country
UK
designer
Mark Pawson
client
Mark Pawson
stock
fluorescent pink paper

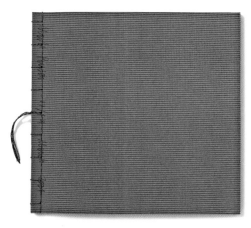

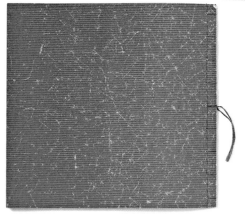

This series of three-dimensional
posters is used to highlight
the all-terrain abilities of a new
bicycle suspension system.
The paper is crumpled to
resemble an aerial view of the
difficult terrain.

country
Singapore
design practice
Kinetic Singapore
designers/art directors
Pann Lim
Roy Poh
client
Single Trek Cycle
printer
Koford Press
stock
art paper 250gsm

30 To add a unique finishing effect to this ethereal brochure for a fashion designer, ten irons were bought and used like printing presses. Apparently it took an iron five minutes to burn through all sixteen pages.

country
USA
design practice
Sagmeister Inc
designer
Julia Fuchs
art director
Stefan Sagmeister
typography
Matthias Ernstberger
client
Anni Kuan
printer/finisher
Jae Kim Printing Company
stock
newsprint

32 To emphasize the 'just like home' atmosphere at the Hans Brinker Budget Hotel the basic greyboard cover of this catalogue was literally embroidered with type and a border to resemble the traditional, hand-sewn samplers that hung on the wall.

country
Netherlands
design practice
KesselsKramer
designers
Erik Kessels
Krista Rozema
client
Hans Brinker Budget Hotel
printer/finisher
Drukkerij Aeroprint
stock
greyboard
machine-coated paper

more paperwork cutting and folding

34 Gently free the corners of
the triangle. Fold the top left
corner down and slide into the
slot opposite.

The multi-layered look of this
'ooooooooooooooooooooooo
oooooooooooooo' book is the
result of direct recycling.
The perforated pages of the
hand-sewn book are the by-
product of the badge-making
process. The build up of
colour, seen through the die-cut
holes, creates an op art effect ■

country
UK
designer
Mark Pawson
client
Mark Pawson
stock
coloured copy paper

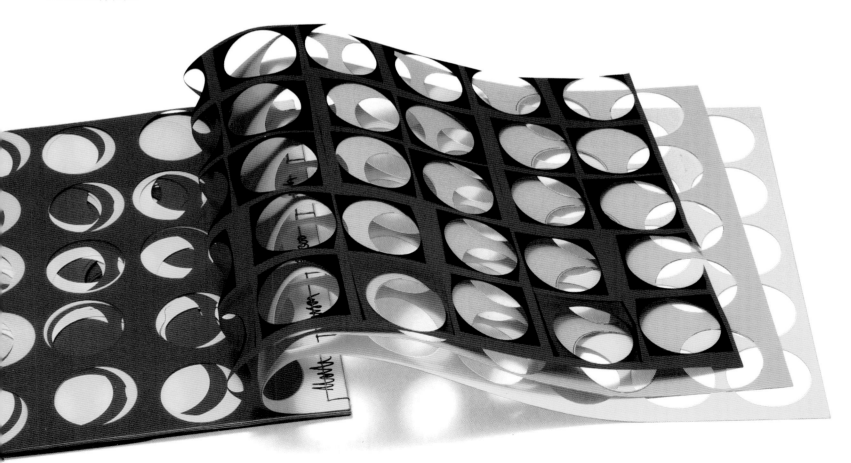

36 This magazine, entitled *spector cut + paste*, questions everything about the way we read and assimilate information. The cover illustrates an article, which looks at the way stereotypes are transmitted through the media and how they are interpreted. A series of printed words, encircled by die-cut discs and emphasized by a UV varnish, can be popped out by the reader to reveal an associated or contrasting word on the page beneath.

country
Germany
designers
Markus Dreßen
Oliver Klimpel
Maria Koehn
printer
Union Druckerei
finisher
Monch OHG
stock
newsprint
matt-coated board

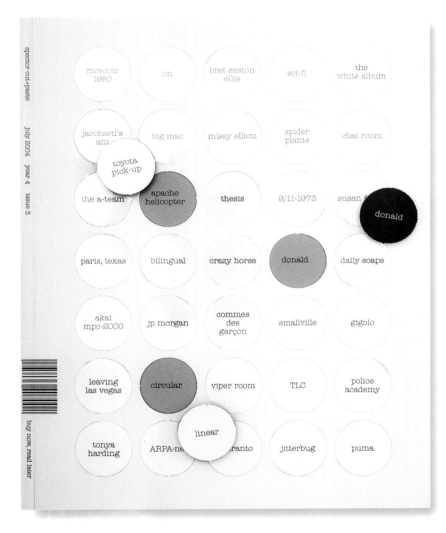

This letter heading has four slots, cut to take one of a series of die-cut business cards. The double-sided cards, which feature images of the company's work, can be placed to cover either Kessels or Kramer, and the receiver can collect an ever growing mini portfolio.

country
Netherlands
design practice
KesselsKramer
designer
Koeweiden-postma
client
KesselsKramer
printer/finisher
Drukkerij Aeroprint
stock
Biotop two-sided satin machine-coated board

Using a format designed by Ray and Charles Eames, these die-cut cards, to promote an interior design company, slot together to build any number of configurations. The slip case bears the logo, which neatly overlays the printed and die-cut initials of the client.

country
UK
design practice
hat-trick design
designers
David Kimpton
Jim Sutherland
art directors
Gareth Howat
David Kimpton
Jim Sutherland
client
Rabih Hage
printer/finisher
Boss Print
stock
slip case: Colorplan Real Grey

lauriergracht 39 / p.o.box 10007 /
1001 ea amsterdam / the netherlands

phone +31(0)20 5301060 /
fax +31(0)20 5301061 / church@kesselskramer.com

KesselsKramer

(print campaign / Diesel)

38

Though this calendar appears to be a one-off collage, it is in fact the result of a painstaking reproduction. What makes it so convincing is the amazingly complex die-cutting that even mimics the torn holes of a page ripped from a note pad and the intricate lace of a doily.

country
Japan
design practice
Draft
designer
Ryosuke Uehara
client
D-BROS
printer/finisher
Taiyo Printing Company
stock
New V matt 81gsm
OK Bright rough 90gsm
Araveal 105gsm

Part of an information pack for an Icograda conference in Nagoya, this die-cut, layered map of the venue really helps to explain the layout of the building, and the exact seating arrangement in the theatre.

country
Japan
design practice
Ken Miki & Associates
designers
Ken Miki
Naoki Ogawa
Shigeyuki Sakaida
art director
Ken Miki
client
Steering Committee, 2003
Icograda Congress Nagoya
stock
matt-coated art

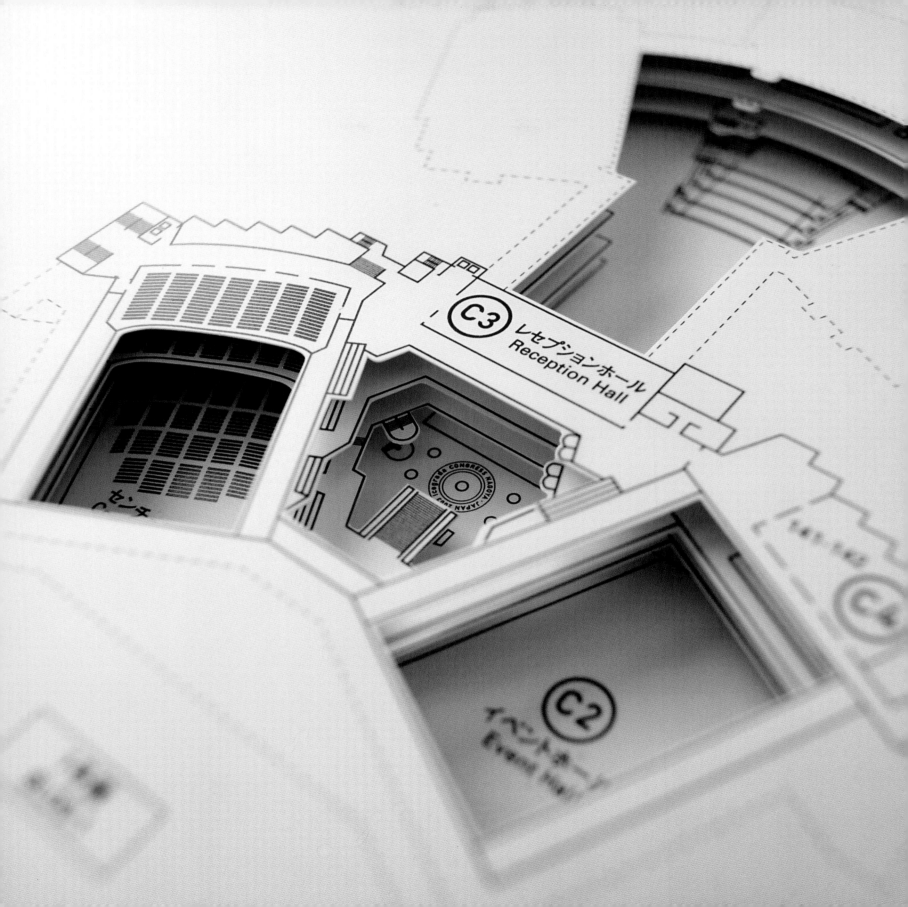

40 These striking greetings cards feature a series of die-cut images that decrease in size on each consecutive layer, giving the cards a three-dimensional appearance.

country
Japan
design practice
Ken Miki & Associates
designer
Ken Miki
client
Fujie Textile Company
stock
cartridge paper

HAPPY BIRTHDAY

HEART TO HEART

This double-sided business card for a designer specializing in digital media uses a combination of cleverly placed die-cut apertures, interlinked with two varying sets of white shapes, to create a different phone number on each side of the card. The holes are reminiscent of the punch cards used by early computers.

country
USA
design practice
Elixir Design
designers
Nathan Durrant
Holly Holmquist
art director
Jennifer Jerde
client
InformationArt
stock
satin-coated card

This elegant range of stationery for art director and designer Debra Zuckerman uses an extremely simple, angled edge enhanced with colour. When folded, it subtly creates the 'Z' of the client's surname.

country
UK
design practice
hat-trick design
designer
Jamie Ellul
art directors
Gareth Howat
David Kimpton
Jim Sutherland
client
Debra Zuckerman
printer/finisher
Boss Print
stock
Zanders Zeta Smooth

42   For this twenty-fifth anniversary book to promote its New York office, Pentagram put together projects it had completed around the city. Minute laser-cut holes, piercing this beautifully subtle cover, pinpoint the locations of the projects and correlate to the client names listed on the page beneath.

country
USA
design practice
Pentagram, New York
designer
Sean Carmody
art director
Paula Scher
client
Pentagram, New York
printer/finisher
Match
stock
matt-coated art

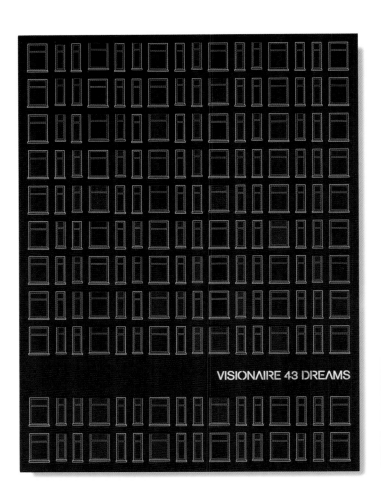

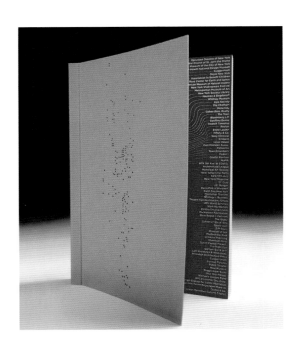

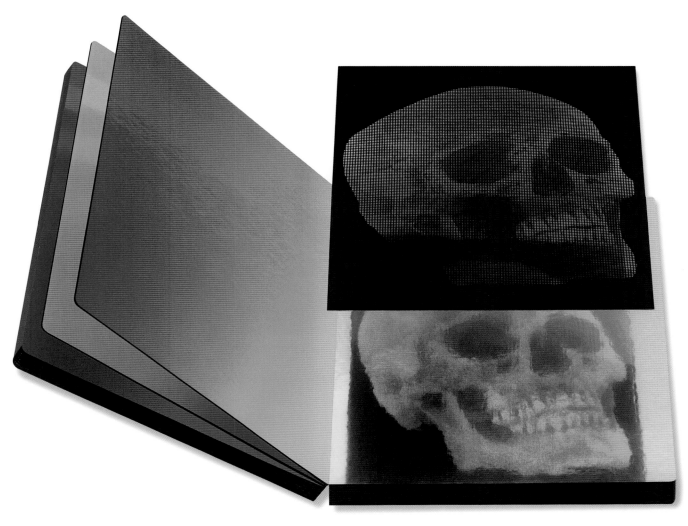

As you can see, a substantial number of high-profile names contributed images to this collection of '43 dreams'. The images have been reproduced using extremely fine laser cutting, which gives them an appropriate ethereal quality. Each work is protected between the leaves of a board book, which is covered with high-gloss paper printed in a rainbow of vivid colours. The book is literally housed in a slip case, which is pierced with laser-cut windows. Contributors include Maurizio Cattelan, Adam Fuss, Roni Horn, Steven Klein, Nick Knight, Karl Lagerfeld, Inez van Lamsweerde & Vinoodh Matadin, Robert Longo, Craig McDean, Simon Periton, David Sims, Mario Sorrenti, Philip Taaffe, Bruce Weber and Rachel Whiteread.

country
USA
designers
Aoife Wasser
Carol Pierre Consorti
art director
Greg Foley
client
Visionaire
stock
black art card 260gsm

44 Described by the designers as
'sculptural paperwork', this
three-dimensional business card
begins life flat. Through a simple
action it turns into a cube, the
surface of which is embossed
with a map of the world, forming
a cubic globe, complete with
the position of the design
company's offices marked with
lines of longitude and latitude.

country
Japan
design practice
Ken Miki & Associates
designer
Ken Miki
client
Ken Miki & Associates
stock
cartridge paper

This fascinating and intricate mailer was designed to explain the Daniel Libeskind proposal for the extension to the Victoria and Albert Museum. When a two-dimensional brochure didn't work the designers decided to go three-dimensional, creating a box that reflected the building's design. When opened, a model of the proposed structure was revealed, along with information about it. The box and model were die-cut and patiently assembled by hand.

country
UK
design practice
johnson banks
client
**Daniel Libeskind Proposal,
Victoria and Albert Museum**
printer/finisher
Fernedge
stock
matt-coated art 400gsm

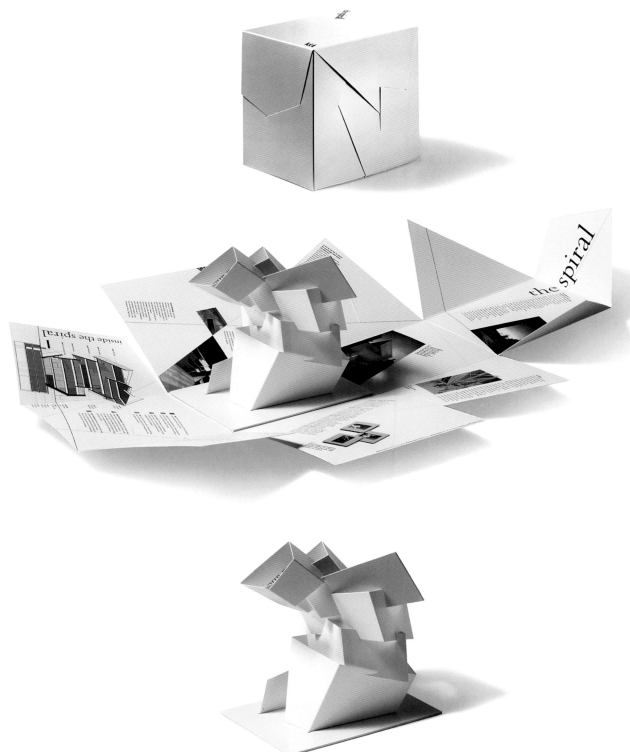

46 This New Year's card, which is both simple and elegant, uses a single thread that passes from the '2' printed on one side, through the centre of the two die-cut '0's, to the back of the card where it connects with the '1' printed there, giving the appearance of a continuous line.

country
Japan
design practice
Ken Miki & Associates
designer
Ken Miki
client
Ken Miki & Associates
stock
matt-uncoated card

This amusing pop-up card uses a cut-out of the monkey's tail on the cover, linked to a duplicate image of the monkey printed on the inside, to give the illusion of movement. He seemingly swings down to grab the red spot when the card is opened.

country
Japan
design practice
Draft
designer
Yoshie Watanabe
client
D-BROS
printer/finisher
Sannichi Printing Company
stock
Felton 198gsm

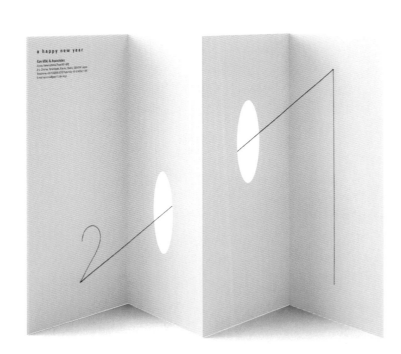

Apparently, the stories of how
this couple first met were too
hot for standard printed type, so
in this wonderful filigree pop-up
wedding announcement there is
no printing. Instead all the type
is burned out of the paper by
laser. The individual stories are
carried on the fine strands,
while, if you peer through the
lace, you are able to read the
details of the wedding.

country
USA
design practice
Sagmeister Inc
designers
Stefan Sagmeister
Matthias Ernstberger
Miao Wang
art director
Stefan Sagmeister
based on design by
Masahiro Chantani
client
Renee & Robert Wong
manufacturers
Joe Freedman
Hestia House
die-cutter
Sarabande Press
stock
Strathmore Writing 350gsm

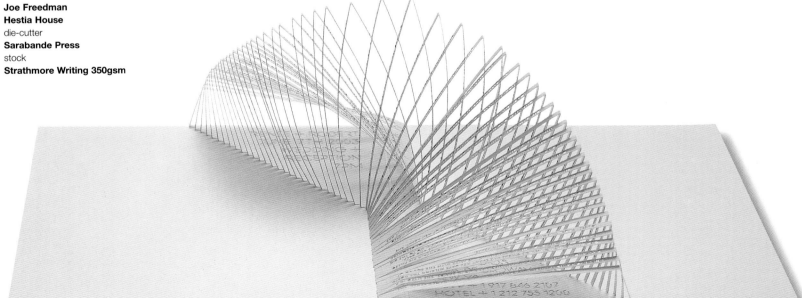

This invitation/poster for an art event, 'Ravaudage urbain', takes the form of a map which plots out the location of activities. To reflect the 'urban deorganized' theme, the poster, which arrived wrapped with tape normally used to cordon off areas, was folded like a map but orientated at 20 degrees – the corners cleverly locked into slots to hold it together. As it is unfolded the irregular die-cut shape becomes apparent, as do seven apertures, representing the exhibiting groups.

country
Canada
design practice
Kolegram
designer
Mike Teixeira
client
Axenéo 7
printers/finishers
St Joseph Corporation
Capital Box
die-cutter
BLM Trade Printers
stock
HannoArt Silk 150gsm

Produced to support this art college's online prospectus, which was lacking in imagery, the brochure comprised thirty-two pages of images with no text. Instead, details relating to the college and its courses are printed on this interestingly folded dust jacket, which doubles as an A2 poster that can be used for career fairs and open days.

country
UK
design practice
MadeThought
designers
Ben Parker
Paul Austin
client
Ravensbourne College of Design and Communication
printer/finisher
Perivan Creative Print
stock
text: Consort Royal Brilliance 170gsm
cover/poster: Kestrel Offset 170gsm

As a visual identity for a series of 'art primers', the designers created a simple but memorable device. A tab, on the return of the covers, projects through a slot which separates the text from the images.

country
UK
design practice
Graphic Thought Facility
designer
Paul Neale
client
Royal Jelly Factory
printer/finisher
Hong Kong Graphics and Printing
stock
text: wood-free paper 150gsm
matt-coated art 150gsm
cover: silk art 250gsm

50 The novel theme for this menu for a paper company's award ceremony was based on the popular child's fortune teller game. The menu was folded and, following tradition, each flap, when lifted, revealed the next course of the meal.

country
UK
design practice
Carter Wong Tomlin
client
Premier Papers
printer/finisher
Ventura Press
stock
Premier Naturalis
Arctic white

What an appealing idea it is to create an invitation that is both informative and functional. Concertina folded, just as we did as children, this fan proved invaluable for guests on the night, at a summer gathering for the British Broadcasting Corporation (BBC).

country
UK
design practice
NB: Studio
designer
Nick Vincent
art directors
Nick Finney
Ben Stott
Alan Dye
client
BBC
printer
Impressions
finisher
DKP Finishing
stock
Challenger Offset 80gsm

An enormous A1 blow up of the company's letterhead was used in this mailer to carry the message 'sending words around the globe'. It was then, appropriately, folded into a giant paper aeroplane, transforming a serious communication into a memorable, larger-than-life toy.

country
UK
design practice
hat-trick design
designers
Gareth Howat
Adam Giles
Jim Sutherland
art directors
Gareth Howat
David Kimpton
Jim Sutherland
client
Verbatim
printer/finisher
Boss Print
stock
Skye Brilliant White

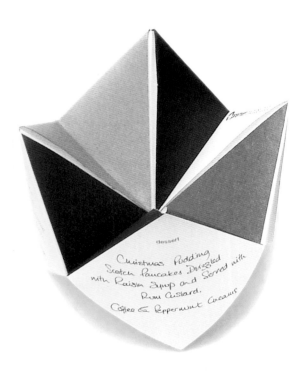

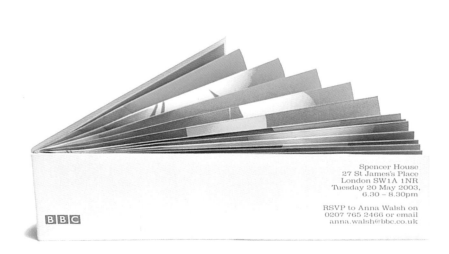

the business of language

52 This radical approach to a catalogue, for an exhibition celebrating 'the book' at the turn of the millennium, works so well it's amazing that it hasn't been done before.

An interesting and original object in its own right, it comprises a series of information posters representing each artist, which were folded to make a leaflet These could be sold individually, or as a set, held in a translucent plastic cover that also acts as a carrier. In a real feat of registration, each leaflet has the artist's name printed in exquisitely small, coloured type along the spine.

country
UK
design practice
SAS
designers
Gilmar Wendt
Matt Tomlin
Frankie Goodwin
client
MakingSpace Publishing
printer/finisher
Perivan Creative Print
stock
brochure: Phoenix
Motion 150gsm
carrier: Velbec Plastic

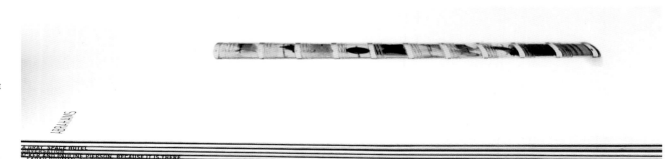

more paperwork binding

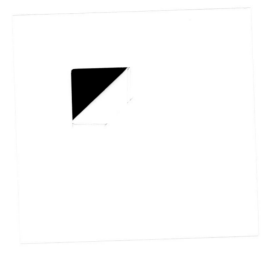

Simple but sumptuous, this sample book and invitation to a launch lets the paper speak for itself. The luscious colours build up to create an attractive pattern that also shows through the lettering of the silkscreened cloth binding. Both the cover and the invitation are laminated or duplexed, taking the weight of the cover up to 1,400gsm, giving them a very satisfying brick-like quality. Inside a real tour de force of printing and finishing techniques was used and a range of colour variations produced, adding to the layered effect.

country
UK
design practice
SEA
designers
Bryan Edmondson
John Simpson
Jamie Roberts
client
GF Smith
printer/finisher
Moore
stock
Colorplan 120, 135, 150, 175, 270, 350, 540, 700gsm

56 The advantage of wiro binding is that you can bind pretty well anything together. This novel annual report, for a tool-hire company, reflects the straightforward, honest nature of the business by employing a range of standard office envelopes to house the text. The information is typed onto the company's fax paper, memo paper and letterheads and inserted into the envelopes ■

country
UK
design practice
NB: Studio
art directors
Nick Finney
Ben Stott
Alan Dye
client
Speedy Hire
printer/finisher
Jones & Palmer
stock
envelopes: C4 self-sealing
Manilla
non-window pocket 90gsm
C4 gummed Manilla window
pocket 90gsm
C4 ungummed Manilla
internal mail, non-window
pocket with 4 holes 120gsm
C4 gummed Manilla
non-window pocket 90gsm
backing board: greyboard
1,000 micron
insert leaves: bond 115gsm

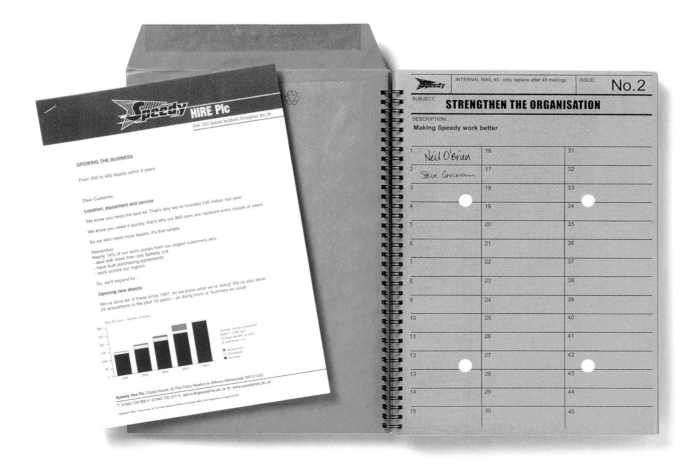

The hand-folded cover of this catalogue for the architecture students at the Royal College of Art, London, opens like a precious parcel, to symbolize the ground on which their work is sited. Pockets formed in the cover, by the construction of the folds, can take other information collected at the show.

country
France
design practice
EricandMarie
designers
Marie Bertholle
Éric Gaspar
client
Royal College of Art, London
printer/finisher
Colortec
stock
matt-uncoated art

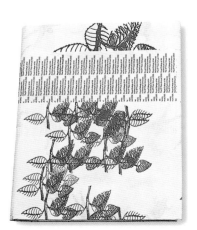

58 Reflecting the approach of this architectural practice, which 'operated outside of existing parameters', art photographers were commissioned to interpret its buildings. The photographic essays were bound using an unusual combination of folds and perforations, to create a cover within a cover.

country
Australia
design practice
Fabio Ongarato Design
designers
Fabio Ongarato
Stefan Pietsch
client
Elenberg Fraser
stock
Parilux 1S gloss white
superfine

To promote a warehouse conversion, several objectives had to be achieved – a high-quality portrayal of the building and its location, the facts, figures and plans required for the agents, and a combination of the two for prospective buyers. One brochure was produced with two distinct elements, using different stock, allowing both the books to be viewed at once. Alternatively, they can be separated using the perforations between the adjoining covers.

country
UK
design practice
Cartlidge Levene
client
Millennium Lofts
printer/finisher
Fulmar Colour
stock
cover: Altura Gloss 380gsm
text: Millennium Real
Art 170gsm
Neptune Unique 150gsm

Structured to encourage
recipients to remember the
name change of this insurance
company, the binding combines
two books, in which the back
cover is common to both.
This approach was devised to
keep the photographic essay
and the text together, but
also independent.

country
Netherlands
design practice
KesselsKramer
designer
Krista Rozema
client
Reaal
printer/finisher
Drukkerij Aeroprint
stock
Yselprint

60 These witty notebooks are
bound together by the simple
use of a rubber band located
in notches top and bottom.
A hand is printed on the reverse
and the rubber band is fixed in
such a way that the hand
appears to be holding onto it.

country
Japan
design practice
Draft
designer
Ryosuke Uehara
client
D-BROS
printer/finisher
Taiyo Printing Company
stock
Fluesand 326gsm

This catalogue for the 'State of Play' exhibition at the Serpentine Gallery, London, is interleaved with a set of twelve postcards. These postcards, taken from the actual exhibition, were printed at the very last minute and inserted into the catalogue. They were held together using a selection of coloured elastic bands, which the printed cover playfully echoes and camouflages.

country
UK
design practice
Boy Meets Girl S&J
designer
Daniel Eatock
client
Serpentine Gallery
printer/finisher
PJ Print
stock
uncoated paper 100gsm

State of Play

Maurizio Cattelan
Martin Creed
Tony Feher
Christian Jankowski
Gabriel Kuri
Bjørn Melhus
Aleksandra Mir
Tim Noble and Sue Webster
Pipilotti Rist
David Shrigley
Andreas Slominski
Sarah Sze

62 To promote George Tsonev's
impressive acrobatic skills
to casting agents, the designers
produced a 'paper George',
a sophisticated flick book.
Cunning use of interleaved
pages of differing lengths
enables you to see one 'flip'
sequence when the book
is flipped forwards and a 'back
flip' sequence when the book
is flipped backwards.
The book is bound with a
black plastic band, reflecting
the flexibility of the acrobat.

country
UK
design practice
The Partners
designers
Tracy Avison
Helen Cooley
Kath Crawford
client
George Tsonev
printer/finisher
CTD Capita
stock
cover: Stardream Silver
two-sided 285gsm
text: Parilux Silk 170gsm

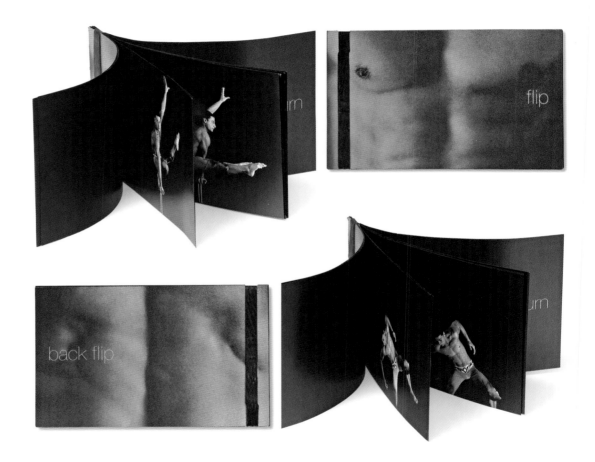

The binding of this book for the Arts & Business/Financial Times Awards adds great drama. To find out the winners, it has to be literally torn open. The cover, which is wrapped around the foredge, the reverse of normal binding, is Singer sewn along the spine. Two lines of perforations on the foredge and a thumb cut facilitated the tearing. Inside it features black and white photography of the award, printed onto clear acetate to reflect its polished perspex.

country
UK
design practice
Radford Wallis
designers/art directors
Stuart Radford
Andrew Wallis
client
Arts & Business
printer/finisher
Empress Litho
printer
acetate: White Crescent
stock
cover: Neptune 350gsm
text: Neptune 300gsm
acetate: clear rigid PVC
140 micron

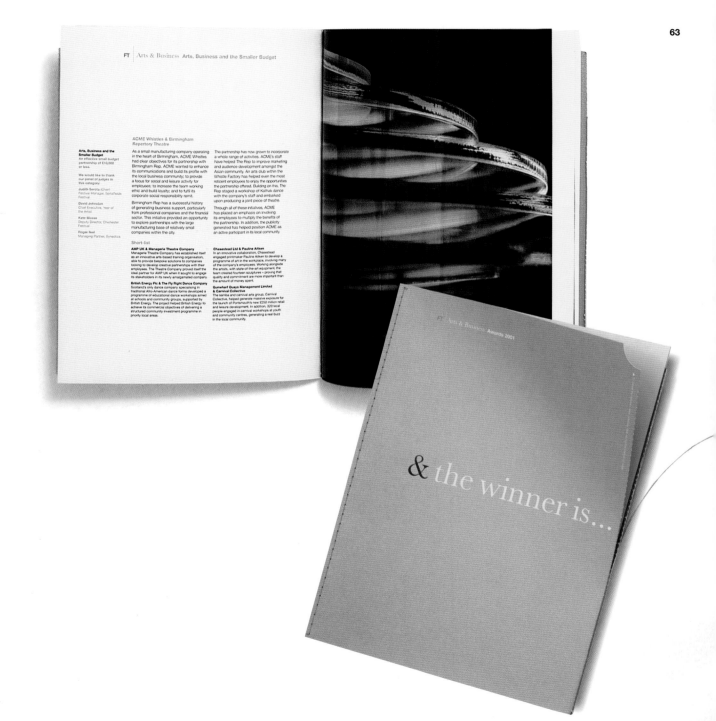

Here the designers certainly achieved their desire to create a binding that emphasized the unusual nature of the work in this exhibition catalogue. Traditional bookbinding techniques are revealed by the short-cut cover, which carries the blind-embossed icon of the exhibition ■

country
Netherlands
design practice
KesselsKramer
designers
Harmine Louwé
Erik Kessels
client
Kunst en Cultuur
Noord-Holland
printer
Drukkerij Plantijn
finisher
Casparie
stock
wood-free offset paper
greyboard

An elegant catalogue for
an exhibition of Wim Crouwel
posters, which uses Swiss
binding. This allows the front
cover to be opened right back,
without creasing, giving a very
refined appearance. The
pages are sewn in folios, and
held together using glue
and a fine cloth around the
spine. The cloth on the back
is then glued onto the inside
back cover. On the cover, an
extremely fine embossing
is miraculously registered with
equally fine outline type.

country
UK
design practice
SEA
designers
Bryan Edmondson
John Simpson
Ryan Jones
clients
Stedelijk Museum
SEA Gallery
printer/finisher
Moore
stock
cover: Naturalis 330gsm
text: Naturalis 160gsm
back section: GF Smith
Biblio 50gsm

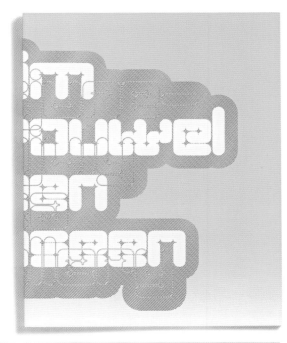

Made of thin, tissue-like paper in
a rich variety of colours, this
calendar uses the transparency
of the paper to provide a work
that changes with the passing of
time. The asymmetry of each
layer allows you to see the
actual colour of the paper as
well as the combined hue.

country
Japan
design practice
Draft
designer
Yoshie Watanabe
client
D-BROS
printer/finisher
Taiyo Printing Company
stock
Kalape 19gsm

Traditional bookbinding techniques have been used in this anything-but-traditional, self-promotional portfolio entitled 'Horizontal/Vertical'. The designers combined both portrait and landscape pages. The dynamic shape of the cover is the result of the juxtaposition of the two.

country
France
design practice
EricandMarie
designers
Marie Bertholle
Éric Gaspar
client
EricandMarie
bookbinder
Ex-Libris, UK
stock
matt-coated art

To convey the uncompromising 'rock and roll' spirit of a new range of Levi's®, every page of this distorted book was cut using a different die, creating this fan effect. The cloth-bound cover is printed in copper, overlayed with turquoise, to give the appearance of oxidization.

country
UK
design practice
The Kitchen
designers
Rob Petrie
Sam Muir
client
Levi Strauss & Co
printer/finisher
Artomatic
stock
high-gloss art 350gsm

68 The dust jacket of this book *Sample*, which features the work of 100 ground-breaking fashion and accessory designers, is quite exquisite. It uses paper as a textile, with fine pencil pleats held in place with a waist band of elastic, to which a label carrying the book title is affixed. Inside, the pages of each signature are cut to different sizes to continue the layered, pleated effect.

country
USA
designer
Julia Hasting
client
Phaidon Press
stock
matt-coated art

more paperwork interactive

These tantalizing 'design-it-yourself' stamps were originally designed as an interactive set for children that, not surprisingly, became as popular with adults. Following in the Mr Potato Head tradition, this set of colourful fruit and vegetable stamps is accompanied by a wonderful kit of body parts and accessories with which you can personalize the stamps – the permutations are endless! Another unusual feature of this set is the kiss-cut shape of the stamp, which partially follows the contour of the fruit.

country
UK
design practice
johnson banks
client
Royal Mail
printer/finisher
Walsall Security Printers
stock
Avery Sass Laminate
Glad Filter Face Paper

72 This bird is the outcome
of an origami set to publicize
Photonica, a photographic
library. Following the descriptor
'play with images', the twenty
sheets of paper in the set
feature photographic images
and come with instructions on
how to make this bird.

country
UK
design practice
NB: Studio
designer
Jodie Wightman
art directors
Nick Finney
Ben Stott
Alan Dye
client
Photonica
stock
bible paper

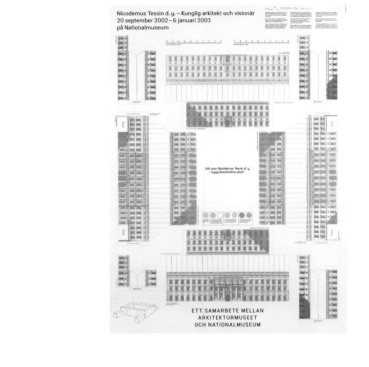

An entertaining poster for an exhibition of the architecture of Nicodemus Tessin the Younger, which can be transformed into one of his buildings. It can be coloured in any one of the three suggested colour schemes from the seventeenth, eighteenth or nineteenth century.

country
Sweden
design practice
Happy Forsman & Bodenfors
art directors
Andreas Kittel
Anders Kornestedt
client
The Swedish Museum
of Architecture
printer/finisher
Billes
stock
Lessebo Linné 250gsm

This humourous self-promotional Christmas card comes in the form of an origami set, branded 'Throw It'. There's everything needed to make an origami snowball – ten sheets of white paper, folding instructions and an 'operating guide'!

country
UK
design practice
NB: Studio
designer
Ramiro Oblitas
art directors
Nick Finney
Ben Stott
Alan Dye
client
NB: Studio
printer/finisher
Principle Colour
stock
bible paper

74   Focusing on the idea that
anything that the company does
is worth remembering, this
annual report features a number
of images that can be cut
out, kept and literally framed
in the cover. An ingenious
integral strut in the the back
cover allows the frame to stand,
wherever you want it.

country
Singapore
design practice
Kinetic Singapore
designers/art directors
Leng Soh
Pann Lim
Roy Poh
client
Amara Singapore
printer/finisher
Colourscan
stock
cover: art card 230gsm
front frame:
art card 420gsm
back stand:
technical board 1mm
concept pages:
art paper 157gsm
financial pages:
wood-free paper 100gsm

Each one of these amazing stamps uses a different process to represent a Nobel prize-winning event or person. Peace uses embossing – a first for a stamp. Literature has a microprinting of a TS Eliot poem. Chemistry uses thermochromic ink, in which heat from your hand reveals an ion trapped within the carbon 60 molecule. Physics uses holographic foil, featuring an image that represents a boron molecule. Physiology or Medicine uses 'scratch and sniff' eucalyptus scent. Economic Science uses intaglio (not shown).

country
UK
design practice
HGV Design
client
Royal Mail
printer/finisher
Joh Enschedé Security Printing, Netherlands
stock
Tullis Stamp Paper

76 The title of this album, 'Fantastic Spikes through Balloons' by Skeleton Key, was the inspiration for the CD cover, featuring photographs of balloon-like objects, including sausages, woopie cushions and blowfish, with a series of die-cut holes punched through them. The band did not want the listeners to be distracted by reading their lyrics while listening to the music, so the words of the songs are printed flipped. They are only readable when seen reflected in the mirrored surface of the CD.

country
USA
design practice
Sagmeister Inc
designers
Stefan Sagmeister
Hjalti Karlsson
art director
Stefan Sagmeister
client
Capitol Records
stock
gloss-coated art 130gsm

Created for an exhibition investigating the role of the book at the turn of the millennium, this project celebrates twelve practical, but potentially redundant, items found in a traditional stationery cupboard and finds new, musical uses for them. The instruments of the 'office orchestra' are contained in a cardboard tube that doubles up as a big bass drum and includes the pen-pipe, castaclips, whine bar, rula-la, staplaphone, corectoracas and elastalute. Each object is accompanied by instructions on musical techniques, the idea being to encourage the office community to collaborate in creating a musical celebration of their environment ∎

country
UK
design practice
SAS
designers
Andrea Chappell
Cherry Goddard
client
MakingSpace Publishing
stock
cardboard tube

78   The challenge for the designers of this promotional piece for a paper company was how to translate the moving images created by Richard Morrison, a leading exponent of film titles, onto the printed page. Their solution was to involve the recipient by making the book into a collection of interactive flick books, possibly the first time this has ever been done. The film clips could then be flicked forwards or backwards to see the image moving, as it did on screen. By a very happy coincidence, the paper company happened to produce a paper called 'motion'.

country
UK
design practice
Atelier Works
designers
Quentin Newark
Glenn Howard
client
GF Smith
printer
Westerham Press
finisher
TTB
stock
PhoeniXmotion Xenon
250gsm, 150gsm

When designing this annual
report for a leading food
company, the designers wanted
to highlight vital information.
They did this by making key
pages of the report interactive.
Some are perforated, while
others are die-cut and entwined
or interlaced, all helping to
emphasize the report's most
significant elements.

country
Croatia
design practice
Bruketa & Zinic
designers
Davor Bruketa
Nikola Zinic
client
Podravka
printers
IBL
MIT
stock
Agripina

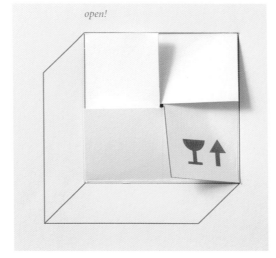
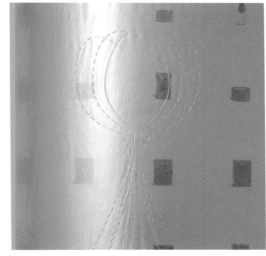

80 It is surprising that the jigsaw format is not used more often, but these greetings cards, shaped like animals, use the technique to great effect. The message is written on the back of the card, which is then broken down to be sent in the accompanying envelope. Great fun, as the recipient has to work out the puzzle both to recognize the animal and to read the message ■

country
Japan
design practice
Draft
designer
Ryosuke Uehara
client
D-BROS
printer/finisher
Sannichi Printing Company
stock
Reporle 81gsm
Felton 140gsm
chipboard 900gsm

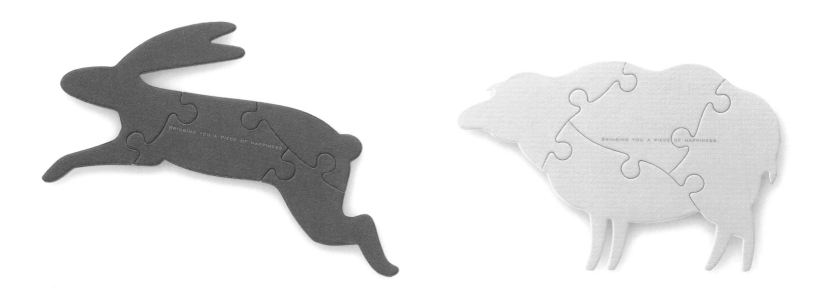

more paperwork mixed media

82

Inspired by a client of this agency which manufactured washing powder, the designers continued the laundry theme with the binding of this promotional piece. The A3 cloth-bound covers were Singer sewn down the spine, incorporating a '100% Press & Poster' satin label, which plays nicely on the theme. The agency's name was blind debossed as a signature.

country
UK
design practice
The Partners
designers
Greg Quinton
Jack Renwick
Helen Cooley
Kath Crawford
client
J Walter Thompson
printer/finisher
Gavin Martin Associates
stock
cloth: Ratchford Windsor Craft
text: Galerie Art Silk 250gsm

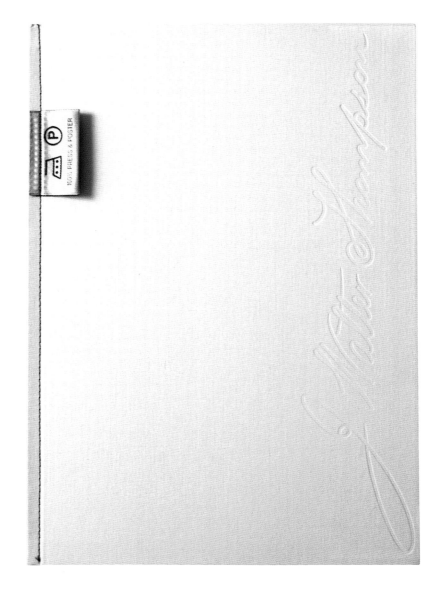

84

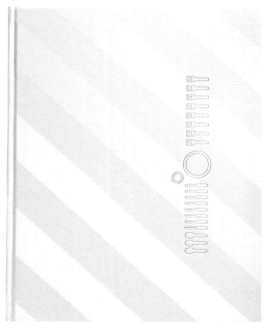

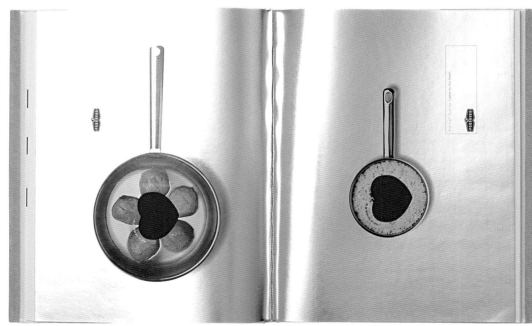

more paperwork mixed media

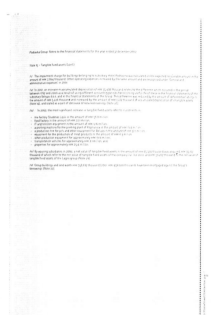

A real tour de force of materials **85**
and techniques, this annual
report for a leading food
company really makes the most
of the food vernacular. The
dust jacket is printed on baking
parchment. The cover uses
damask tablecloth for its binding
and is foil blocked with cutlery.
Inside you can cook the heat-
sensitive hearts – the company
symbol – which are printed onto
silver foil. The accounts are
bound with perforated French
folds that can be torn open,
to reveal the recipes of the
products responsible for
the figures.

country
Croatia
design practice
Bruketa & Zinic
designers
Davor Bruketa
Nikola Zinic
client
Podravka
printers
IBL
MIT
stock
baking parchment
Agripina

COOKED VEAL KNEEPAD

1 veal kneepad, 15 dg carrots, 10 dg celery, 1 smaller cabbage, 50 dg potatoes, 1 tomato, grains of pepper, salt, 2 dl dry white wine, 1 bundle of parsley leaves, tbs. Vegeta. The kneepad cut in half put into the boiling water and boil shortly. Throw out the water and put the kneepad to cook into 2 l of water, add salt, pepper and Vegeta. Let it simmer till it is half cooked. Add tomato, celery and carrots cut into stripes, and continue to cook. After about ten minutes add potatoes cut into slices, and cabbage cut into stripes. Cook till it is done, and remove meat from the bone, arrange it with cooked vegetables in a deeper dish, pour with soup and sprinkle with cut parsley.

WINE GOULASH

50 dg beef, 4 onions, 6 dg tomato concentrate Podravka, 2 dl wine, 20 dg potatoes, 4 tbs. oil, salt, ground red pepper, laurel, caraway, 1 tbs. Vegeta. Cut the meat into equal pieces and fry it shortly on heated oil. Add cut onions and continue to stew adding occasionally water or soup. Add laurel, caraway, Vegeta, and before it is done add a little salt if needed. Add ground red pepper, tomato concentrate, wine and potatoes cut into squares. Cook until the meat and the potatoes are tender.

86

To herald the move to a new
studio, this design practice
revamped its identity, which is
based on the ticker tape form
of their name. Wherever it
appears, it is punched out and
is accompanied by a matrix
of dots that surround or back it.
The consequential layering
is achieved in different ways
on each piece. The letterhead
has dots printed front and
back in varying hues. On the
business card the dots are
etched to different levels, while
on the polypropylene portfolio
they are reversed out of silkscreened silver.

country
UK
design practice
Form
designers
Paul West
Paula Benson
Nick Hard
client
Form
printers
stationery: Good News Press
business card:
Photofabrication
portfolio inserts: Le Scott
portfolio: Design East
stock
stationery: Courier Super
Wove 105gsm
business card: stainless
steel 302 0.125mm
portfolio inserts: Consort
Royal Silk 250gsm
portfolio: polypropylene

Containing a photographic essay featuring Tokyo's Tsukiji fish market, this stylish mailer for the photographer was designed to resemble a tuna can. An embossed 'tin lid' was applied to the cover of the board book and the edges were silvered to complete the illusion.

country
UK
design practice
The Partners
designers
Greg Quinton
Dana Robertson
Tony de Ste Croix
photographer
Marcus Lyon
client
Marcus Lyon
printer
Gavin Martin Associates
manufacturer
Graphic Metal Company
stock
cover: aluminium

88 To mark the centenary of this company, the designers were commissioned to create a gift for its employees. Concentrating on their clients' desire 'to make the world a better place', their solution was to involve the recipient by producing an interactive book. This is accompanied by a packet of seeds, contained in a plastic case that ingeniously doubles as a fully functioning watering can. The concept, text and production was in conjunction with Signum Niehe events.

country
Netherlands
design practice
Lava
designers
Yke Bartels
Heike Dehning
Hans Wolbers
Hugo Zwolsman
case: Henk Stallinga
client
Dutch State Mines
printer
Drukkerij Koenders &
Van Steijn
binder
Hepadru
stock
Colorado 90 120gsm
Ensocoat 190gsm
Eurobulk 90 135gsm
Hello Silk 135gsm
Hello Gloss 135gsm
Reviva 115gsm
cover: cardboard 2mm

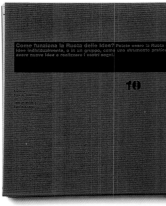

Housed in a case to look like a car handbook, this identity manual for Ford is both appropriate and functional. The cover is embossed, using heat to embed the witty warning into the plastic. Inside, the back cover of the standard printed manual was slipped into a pocket and held in place.

country
UK
design practice
The Partners
designers
Gillian Thomas
Nick Clark
Nigel Davies
Nick Eagleton
Kath Crawford
client
Ford Motor Company
manufacturer
cover: Folders Galore
stock
cover: 'Touch'-style rubber

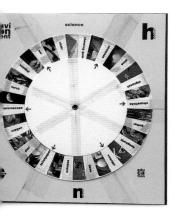

90 This book, for a retrospective exhibition of architects Diller+Scofidios' work, echoes their ideas on 'context, surveillance and the public/private space'. Intended to blur the line between real and simulated events, the cover uses a lenticular process to create an image that changes when tilted. Within the French folds lurks a subtext, accessed by tearing the page via the central thumb cut.

country
USA
design practice
Pentagram, New York
designers
Abbot Miller
Johnschen Kudos
art director
Abbot Miller
client
Whitney Museum of American Art
printer
Steidl
stock
Xenon 115gsm

At a time of economical uncertainty, this striking annual report was designed to convey the concept of growth. Vivid plant imagery and ascending typography were both used to reinforce this idea, but the main feature of this report is undoubtedly the lustrous Astro turf fixed to the cover.

country
Singapore
design practice
Kinetic Singapore
designers/art directors
Leng Soh
Pann Lim
Roy Poh
client
Amara Singapore
printer
Colourscan
stock
financial pages:
wood-free paper 100gsm
review pages:
art paper 157gsm
cover: art card 260gsm
Astro Turf

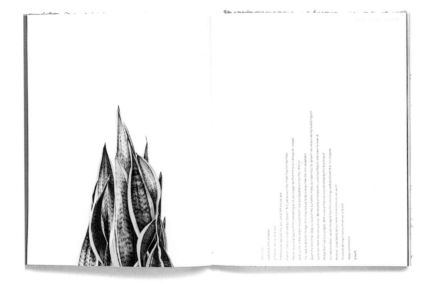

Paper, long seen as the stock-in-trade of the graphic designer, is quite rightly taking its place alongside the myriad of materials available to designers working in the third dimension. There has been an exponential growth in its employment in recent years, as designers of all disciplines recognize the potential that paper can offer. Product designers, fashion designers and architects alike are finding new ways to exploit the properties of paper.

The very stuff that we thought of as ephemeral is now being used to create things of great strength and surprising longevity – products, furniture and even buildings. It is hard to imagine a piece of jewellery or a home for a pet that is made out of paper, let alone a pavilion for Expo 2000, but it has been done – paper is capable of that.

As already mentioned, the longevity of the Japanese paper industry, allied to its ingenuity, has led to paper being deemed unequivocally a valuable, useful and essential material. The Japanese do not set artificial boundaries in the applications of paper. Hence the dominance of ground-breaking designs in the third dimension from Japan. They have even developed a car, the interior and exterior of which are constructed from washi, Japanese paper. However, that is not to say that the rest of the world is without creativity when it comes to paper – far from it. Designers in the West are now realizing that paper is capable of nearly anything. This trend may well have been facilitated by the increasing number of multi-disciplinary design practices around the world, as well as by the determination of some designers to broaden their repertoire and ignore the preconceived boundaries associated with their individual profession.

Designers are not only using paper in its usual finished form – sheets, cardboard tubes, and so on – but are working increasingly with paper recycled in a variety of ways. Papier mâché, for example, has been taken to new limits, from its most basic and ubiquitous form, the humble egg box, to being rediscovered as an art form. Although in Victorian times papier mâché was used to create the finest and most delicate of pieces, they were often totally unrecognizable as paper, covered and decorated as they were with layers of lacquer and intricate painted patterns. Today it is taking on a totally different, and more honest, guise as hero of the piece, often totally unadorned but with a rugged beauty none the less.

94 As well as being used for the end product, paper also plays a valuable role as part of the design process. Because of its flexibility and strength, paper is the perfect material for architectural models. Some of the world's most extraordinary buildings owe their gravity-defying shapes to the qualities of paper that architects have been able to harness.

architecture Paper has long played a vital role in architecture. One of the first steps in the design process, for many architects, is to create a model in paper. Some of these models have a sculptural and ethereal quality and are beautiful in their own right. Other architects have taken this process one stage further and developed a whole system for designing buildings that is centred around utilizing the properties of paper, cutting and folding shapes to inform the ultimate design.

With the exception of interior use – the Japanese shoji screen and, of course, wallcoverings – paper has not been considered as a building material until relatively recently. Lurking under the surface of many a door lies a honeycomb of paper, while large cardboard tubes are often used to cast columns. However, architect Shigeru Ban, the main exponent of paper-based buildings, is bringing the material to the fore. He has developed a range of unique building systems using predominantly paper. Attracted to the material by its low cost, natural colour, accessibility and recyclability, he has designed whole buildings using specially developed waterproofed paper and paper tubes. These factors have been a great asset in much of the work Ban has done for temporary housing in natural disaster areas. He has also produced buildings of great elegance and beauty using the same techniques. Lamination is the key to the strength that the buildings require, the principle of the construction of a paper tube.

Though Ban is without doubt the champion of the paper building, paper structures are being designed by other practices. For example, the 'Local Zone', one of the main exhibition buildings in the Millennium Dome, was designed by Spence Associates, with Ban and Philip Gumuchdjian as consultants. And an extension to a school in Essex – the south wall and roof of which take their lead from origami folds – designed by Cottrell and Vermeulen, has also been constructed using primarily paper-based products. Interestingly, when compressed, the pattern of the stress marks on the paper tubes used for the building apparently follow those of origami folds.

exhibition and sculpture This is an area in which the boundaries between art, design and craft are often blurred. Paper sculpture, for example, popular in the Fifties and Sixties and used extensively in design at the time, has by and large been side-lined in recent years. However, that now appears to be changing. The mood at the moment means that creative people are not so quick to discard a whole genre, but will look at all possibilities. With this attitude, great things are created.

Unlike paper sculpture, origami has gone from strength to strength over its comparatively short, four-century existence. There are now associations all over the world dedicated to origami. It is difficult to imagine that it could get any more intricate or refined, but you may be amazed at how it has developed. Western influences are making their mark too. In some cases it is hard to believe that a single piece of paper can be folded so many times. In fact, it is a widely accepted rule of thumb, that a piece of paper cannot be folded in half more than seven times, but many modern examples of origami seem to defy this.

As well as folded origami, there is kirigami, or architectural origami, which uses a combination of cutting and folding. Exponents of this intricate art, such as Masahiro Chantani, are able to construct mind-blowing structures, very often used for greetings cards, which pop up from the flat to recreate famous buildings, fanciful architectural structures or breathtaking flowers. The designs are so inspiring that followers spend hours copying the forms from books and then proudly display them on the Internet.

As well as exhibitions, featuring astonishing paper sculpture techniques, this section also includes some dynamic window displays. Although this book concentrates on design, it is often difficult to draw a line, so one may see items in this section that are not to be expected. They have been included because they are inspirational and, for that reason, can and do have a connection with design.

fashion and accessories Most of us have been under the misapprehension that the first paper clothes were the disposable paper dresses and knickers of the Sixties. However, in both China and Japan, they have been producing paper clothing for centuries. In fact, some people now believe that paper was not first produced as a writing material, but for a number of other functions, including clothing. This first form of paper, dating from around 100 BC, was made in China from pounded hemp fibres and, though the process was very similar to that of papermaking, the end product was more akin to felt than writing paper. Evidence of this has been discovered recently in China, where a paper hat, belt and shoe were uncovered, dating back to 418 AD.

Several centuries later in Japan, during the Kamakura and the more recent Edo periods, paper kimonos were being manufactured that were considered extremely stylish and were as exclusive and expensive as silk ones. In fact, during formal Shinto ceremonies, the priest still wears a paper robe and a lacquered paper headdress.

There are two types of paper fabric produced in Japan. One uses a lamination of papers that are then manipulated to soften the material. The other, shifu, uses fine shreds of paper twisted to form a yarn, which is then woven. The latter technique is still being used today and produces a fabric that is crisp, light and breathable, rather like linen, and is capable of being washed and reused. Although it has mostly been used to produce expensive clothing, an exhibition of more affordable clothing made from this material has recently toured Japan.

Generally, when it comes to paper in fashion, one tends to think of the paper patterns used as a guide for cutting out cloth. However, paper itself is now playing a leading role. Many fashion design courses around the world incorporate a paper-based design module in their curriculum. Although these exercises are intended to start the student thinking about the qualities and properties of various materials, they have obviously proved an inspiration to many students who have gone on to concentrate on producing final designs in paper. Hussein Chalayan, for example, built a whole collection around paper and magnets. In this book you can see examples of the wonderful and diverse clothes that can be produced from paper, from diaphanous, lace-like dresses to beautiful and delicate wedding dresses, as well as striking sculptural clothes that have all been fashioned in paper.

If clothes can be made of paper then it stands to reason that accessories can, too. Wendy Ramshaw, the eminent jewellery designer, recently produced a book of paper jewellery that one could pop out and wear. By and large the paper is used for decoration but, in some examples, paper is cut and folded to create beautiful and elaborate body adornments that are redolent of an Elizabethan ruff.

packaging This is one aspect of three-dimensional design in which one expects to see paper being exploited. However, it is very often the simplest and subtlest of designs that use paper to best effect – a simple well-placed cut-out to reveal the product, a multiple layering of a card that is generally used individually, or an elegant wrapping. It is also interesting when techniques naturally associated with two-dimensional design are used, such as laser-cutting and blind embossing.

In an age of fast food and throw-away packaging it is good to see that beautifully crafted and detailed objects are still being produced. Indeed, the carrier bag has almost taken on the status of the Gucci handbag, with many people eager to be seen carrying the right one. It's amazing how the outer wrapping can add value and make the object – even a diamond ring – seem more precious. The very fact that many shops now offer the service of gift wrapping shows how important the presentation of an item is to people – and very often it is only for the purchaser.

96   **product** In Japan paper, due to its inherent strength, has long been used to produce a variety of products – bags, fans, kites, lanterns, masks, umbrellas, tarpaulins and, of course, shoji screens and windows. In Korea, furniture was traditionally made from lacquered paper, and oiled paper was used for both floor covering and boat sails. In India a technique of lacquering papier mâché was developed, which enabled the manufacture of fine decorative bangles, boxes and vases. In Persia paper was used for plates and boxes of varying kinds. These items were exported to Western Europe and America where the techniques were adopted to produce a host of items including clock cases, dolls' heads, furniture and architectural decorative moldings. Miraculously, a Dresden watchmaker even produced a timepiece entirely made from paper and papier mâché! However, this productive period was relatively short and, by the end of the nineteenth century, paper products were very much in decline. One product that did buck the trend was the Lloyd Loom range of furniture that has traditionally graced many a bathroom or garden. Still popular today, its main constituent is paper.

While the Akari light sculptures, designed by Isamu Noguchi during the Fifties and Sixties, have become icons of that era, the point at which designers' attention was drawn to paper is likely to be the inspired work of architect Frank O Gehry. His two collections of cardboard furniture, starting in 1972 with 'Easy Edges' – featuring his 'Wiggle' chair which is still in production – and followed by 'Experimental Edges', took a whole new look at the use of paper, highlighting the exciting potential of this modest material. His work, I believe, has encouraged product and furniture designers, fuelled by the interest in all things recycled and environmentally friendly, to investigate what paper and cardboard are capable of. And, because there are no expensive production techniques involved, no injection moulds or die-castings, designers tend to be more lateral when designing with paper.

Particularly striking is the incredible diversity of the outcomes produced using the same raw material, from the most delicate and intricate, multi-layered paper light fitting to an elegant chaise longue and a robust, utilitarian home for a pet.

more paperwork architecture

98 Gently free the corners of this
die-cut square. Gradually crease
along the score lines, so that the
two above and below the centre
line come towards you, while all
others fold away from you.

While many architects use paper for their model making, this architect has developed an approach to design centred around the exploitation of the qualities of paper. As well as teaching her techniques at the architectural faculty of Delft University, she has published an article, 'Folding as a morphogenetic process in architectural design', and *Folding Architecture*, a book which demonstrates her techniques. Here, and on the following page, is the initial stage of a project for the transport hub of a small neighbourhood centre. This illustration of her method has been devised especially for this book, and is based on part of a competition entry executed in conjunction with Giuseppe Mantia.

country
Greece/Netherlands
architect
Sophia Vyzoviti
client
Europan 5

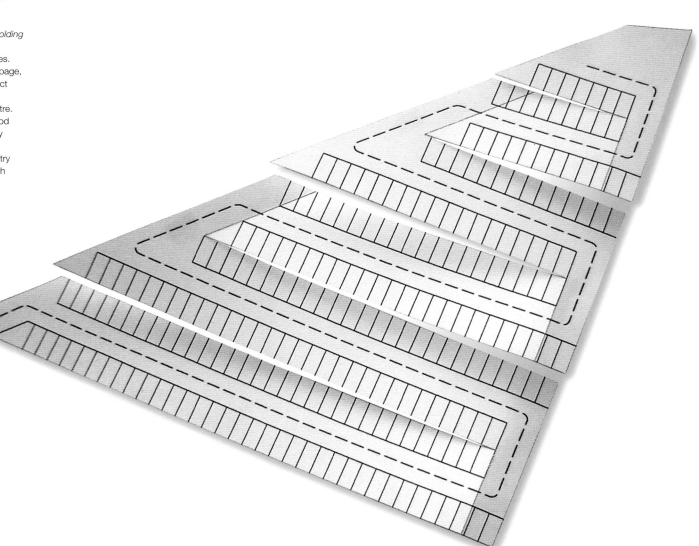

100

paperfold *The result of the process of folding paper, and the product of a folding performance investigated as a generative diagram in architectural design.*
In this case we demonstrate the function of a paperfold prototype as a spatial and organizational diagram in the process of solving a specific design problem.

meander *The meander pattern, which is illustrated here as a paperfold prototype, if scored, cut and unfolded, expands the paper's surface while maintaining its continuity in an enfolding strip.*
This prototypical property of the meander is applied in the constraints of a given site and programme, the design of a park and ride station and shopping centre on a plot adjacent to a public transport interchange hub.
Two properties of the unfolded meander applicable here are: the extended length of path, which is efficient in serving maximum parking spaces while given a minimum inclination of five per cent, produces a three-dimensional surface, a continuous oblique drive and park strip.
The opportunity for a double-orientation surface, inclined along the generative path, which meanders within the perimeter of the given triangular site, and along the length of the site, where it reaches its maximum height gradually. The meander surface operates in two ways, as an oblique ground upon which vehicles and pedestrians coexist in a slow-speed traffic landscape and as a figure, an interior enclosed by the ascending, inclined continuous strip that contains the shopping and neighbourhood facilities. The performance of the meander surface as an architectural prototype that merges figure with ground is evident in the allocation of the given programme in a compact stratified organization.
Sophia Vyzoviti

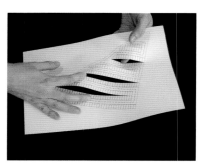

The award-winning design of this after-school club and community centre was driven by the idea of sustainability and based on the inherent strength created by origami folds. Ninety per cent of the building materials are recycled or recyclable and predominantly paper based. The pupils were involved in the design process and collected card, which was recycled to fabricate building components. While their images decorate the columns inside, the outside continues the origami theme, depicting instructions on how to make the locally familiar heron ∎

country
UK
architectural practice
Cottrell and Vermeulen
consulting engineers
Buro Happold
contractor
CG Franklin
origami heron illustrations
Simon Patterson
client
Westborough Primary School
manufacturers
paper and board: Paper Marc
paper tubes: Essex Tube
Windings
panel products: Quinton and
Kaines
materials
recycled newspaper pin board
and structural board
recycled paper tubes
recycled laminated cardboard
honeycomb panels

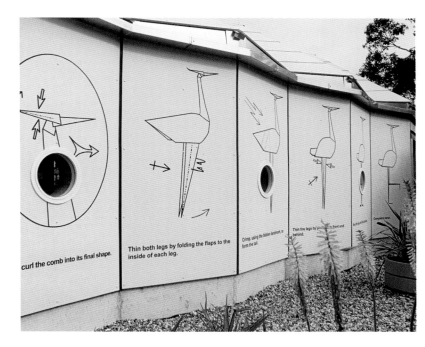

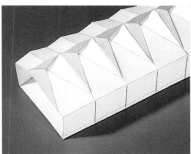

102

Built to house the people left homeless following earthquakes in Kobe during 1995, these paper log houses were the ideal solution, cheap and easy to construct, and warm and pleasing. Taking a slightly ad hoc approach, the houses were built by volunteers on a foundation of beer crates and constructed from 4mm-thick paper tubes. Self-adhesive sponge tape held the tubes together and sealed them from rain. The houses proved so successful that adaptations of them were also used in disaster areas in Turkey and India ■

Designed to be reused, this graceful church and community centre were also built for the refugees at Kobe using the same guiding principles. While the building is curtained with polycarbonate panels, the main feature is undoubtedly the magnificent paper-tube columns, which create the internal space and support the tent-like roof ■

country
Japan
architectural practice
Shigeru Ban Architects
structural engineers
**houses: Hinoru Tezuka,
TSP Taiyo, Eiichiro Kaneko
church: Gengo Matsui,
Shuichi Hoshino, TSP Taiyo,
Mihoko Uchida**
materials
**recycled paper tubes
polycarbonate panels
PVC tent membrane**

Although this elegant, gravity-defying Museum for Children's Art at Nemunoki is not made entirely from paper, the majority of the roof structure is. Special honeycomb board was fabricated, using extra internal gluing which provides additional strength. This then sandwiches plywood to provide the main building component for the structure. The hexagonal roof pattern is achieved by means of specially designed aluminium brackets and is supported by steel columns. Interestingly, this form of paper honeycomb structure has also been approved by the German Minister of Construction ■

country
Japan
architectural practice
Shigeru Ban Architects
structural engineers
Van Structural Design
contractor
TSP Taiyo
client
Mariko Miyagi
materials
paper honeycomb board
plywood
aluminium brackets
steel columns

'Environment' was the theme of Hanover's Expo, and appropriately the concept for this inspirational Japanese pavilion was to create a structure that could be recycled once dismantled. Conceived as a purely paper structure, Ban, who considers paper to be a high-tech material, had to compromise due to pressures from the German authorities. Despite that, this wonderful structure is predominantly paper. The roof, comprising 440 recycled paper tubes, 20 metres long, was constructed over a period of three weeks, from the top down, and raised by a manual jack as additional tubes were added. Internal walls used the same construction as the museum project and the outside was covered in a water- and flame-resistant paper, specially developed by Ban. The circle was satisfactorily completed, as the tubes were bought and recycled by a German paper tube manufacturer ∎

country
Japan
architectural practice
Shigeru Ban Architects
architectural consultant
Otto Frei
structural engineers
Buro Happold
contractor
Takenaka Europe
client
**Japan External
Trade Organization**
manufacturer
Sonoco Europe
materials
**recycled paper tubes
paper honeycomb board
paper membrane**

108 Sustainability, was the concept behind the 'Shared Ground' project, housed in the Millennium Dome, London. A nationwide appeal was launched through the BBC's 'Blue Peter' series for television, asking children to donate five pieces of card, which were recycled to make 100 structural paper tubes. These, along with high-tension cables, honeycomb panels and louvres of recycled paper, were used to create this dynamic spiralling structure. A complementary educational programme was developed and the building was to be ultimately repulped, to reinforce the theme ■

country
UK
architectural practice
Spence Associates
collaborating architects
Gumuchdjian Associates
architectural consultant
Shigeru Ban
structural engineers
Buro Happold
contractor
Mivan
client
NMEC
manufacturer
tubes: Sonoco Europe
materials
recycled paper tubes
paper honeycomb board
paper louvres

110   Free the corners of the square
carefully. Gently pinch along
either side of the diagonal curve
and then ease the top right-
hand corner down to locate
into the angled notch.

To encourage people, in the Swedish 'year of architecture', to take more interest in their buildings, the designers conceived these cardboard frames, mounted on lamposts around the city. It's amazing how successful the simple aperture is in drawing the eye up to see what is visible through it.

country
Sweden
design practice
Happy Forsman & Bodenfors
designer
Gavin Smart
art director
Anders Kornestedt
client
The Swedish Museum of Architecture
printer/finisher
Aare
stock
satin-coated art paper laminated onto greyboard

MITSUKOSHI

To promote the twisted pleats of 'Dragon Dance', a new product from Issey Miyake, a series of window displays was developed. Traditional paper-lantern techniques were used to create dramatic and energetic dragon-like shapes. The plasticized paper was printed, cut and folded, and supported with the help of fine wires.

country
Japan
design practice
Sayuri Studio
designer
Sayuri Shoji
client
Issey Miyake
stock
Yupo 820gsm

Built to promote the launch of a new shampoo, this monumental structure comprised over 1,300 boxes. The same box, filled with product samples, was presented to guests at the launch event.

country
Japan
designers
**display: Sayuri Studio
gift box: Akiko Jinnai,
Sayuri Shoji**
client
FT Shiseido Company
stock
pearlized cover stock

These exquisite creations are
surprisingly not made from
fabric. Inspired by a catalogue
from the Kyoto Costume
Institute entitled 'Revolution in
Fashion', painter and designer
Isabelle de Borchgrave decided
to recreate some of the dresses
using paper – her stock in
trade. It soon became a passion
and, in collaboration with
costumier Rita Brown,
she has interpreted costumes
from museums around the
world. These are certainly
not reproductions and it is the
transition into paper, and
the way in which paint is applied
to give the impression of lace or
fabric, that makes the costumes
so imposing. This is a small
part of a stunning collection that
has recently travelled the globe.

country
Belgium/Canada
designer
Isabelle de Borchgrave
costumier
Rita Brown
exhibition
Papiers à la Mode, travelling
stock
pattern-making paper
corrugated board
lense paper

116 These wonderful sculptural books are inspired by the volumes from which we gather the knowledge of life.
The architectural shapes are created by folding the pages of reference books in a number of ways; some feature hardbacks, some paperbacks. In some instances the book blocks are rebound and distorted to create new forms, while in others the pages are set free to create a collection of origami butterflies.
All emphasize the qualities of the paper and, however the books are manipulated, the knowledge within remains constant ∎

country
UK
designer
Jennie Farmer
client
Jennie Farmer
material
found books

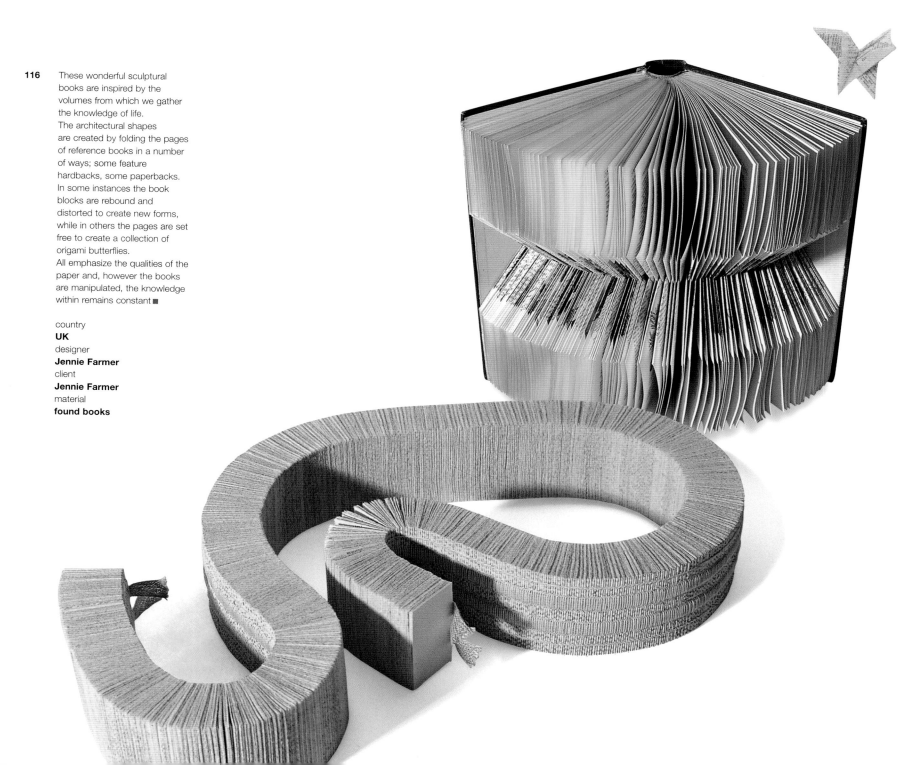

Created for an exhibiton entitled 'Water', this small sculpture uses a selection of mineral-water labels, cut to represent sea anemones, which were wrapped around magnets, enabling the arrangment to be changed ■

country
Switzerland
designer
Sonja Trachsel
exhibition
L´eau, The Market of Applied Arts, Lausanne
materials
paper mineral-water labels
tin
magnets

These 'brick book' installations were created to celebrate the importance, and fundamental nature, of the book as a unit of knowledge. Employing traditional bookmaking techniques, such as slip case construction and painted edges, the books were used to build a variety of structures, or 'libraries'.

country
USA
design practice
Pentagram, New York
designer
Abbott Miller
client
Kiosk
exhibition
Brick/Book, Andrea Rosen Gallery
printer/finisher
Studley Press
stock
cover: Fox River Crushed Leaf 80#
text: Fox River Coronado 60# Smooth White

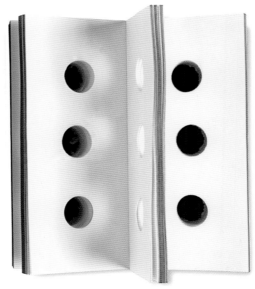
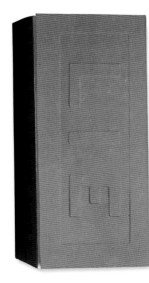

120 This fascinating paper sculpture uses skills and techniques that are rarely seen. While this artist also designs large-scale works, this is made from humble copy paper. The 'Impenetrable Castle' emerges miraculously from the surface of a single flat sheet of paper.

country
Denmark
designer
Peter Callesen
exhibition
Gallery Koch und Kesslau, Berlin
stock
copy paper 80gsm

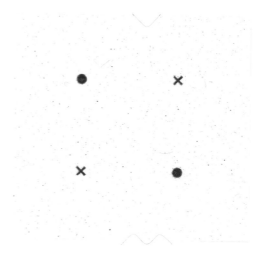

122

Part of the 'Unfinished' collection from the Kyote Costume Institute, a gift of Comme des Garçons, these delicate lace-like dresses use a traditional Japanese cut-out technique to stencil patterns onto cloth. Here the stencil becomes the dress itself, symbolizing the theme of the collection.

country
Japan
designer
Rei Kawakubo, Comme des Garçons Noir
exhibition
Kyote Costume Institute
material
Japanese stencil paper

124

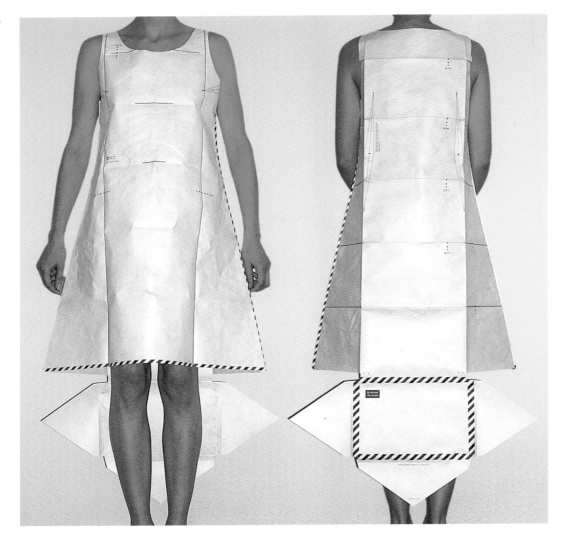

This witty and, believe it or not, washable dress combines the vernacular of a paper dress-making pattern with an airmail letter, complete with fitting instructions. A set of stickers were included for securing the darts, to improve the fit and to seal the package. The envelope train was perforated so that the wearer could remove it, if preferred.

country
UK
designers
fashion: Hussein Chalayan
graphics: rebecca and mike
client
Hussein Chalayan
material
Tyvek®

Commissioned by a British tabloid, this sensational wedding dress is suitably constucted from more than 250 florets of folded newspaper, which are sewn together. The marriage of pleats and images creates a sumptuously rich visual texture ■

country
UK
designer
Rachael Sleight
client
The Sun,
News Group Newspapers
material
recycled newspapers

To address the imbalance between the cost of the average wedding dress and its single appearance, the designer of this wonderful dress decided to use paper, which happily represents the first year of marriage.
The bride is able to personalize her dress, which comes flat packed, by selecting from a collection of skirt, bodice, bustle and flower designs. For even more economy, offcuts from the lace pattern punched in the skirt can be used as confetti.

country
UK
designer
Rachael Sleight
client
Rachael Sleight
materials
skirt: Fabriano Spa
cartridge 120gsm
Japanese paper and ribbon
corset: crêpe paper
bustle and flowers:
Fabriano Spa
cartridge 120gsm

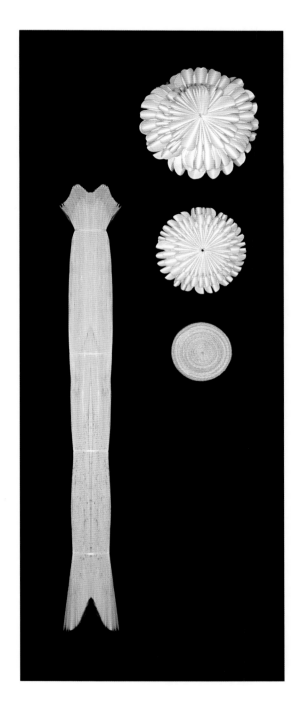

128 The work of this multi-
disciplinary designer centres
around paper and paper
substitutes. The 'body vest' on
the left is sculpted from paper,
handmade from linen fibres.
Judicious cutting allows the
paper bodice to fit the form of
the body, while the natural
edges of the paper become a
decorative feature.
The 'cut dress' opposite is
based on a framework of
Tyvek®, which has been
randomly interwoven with fine
strands of the same material.

country
UK
designer
Kei Ito
client
Kei Ito
materials
vest: handmade linen paper
dress: Tyvek®

130 This designer uses paper in a precious, jewel-like way. This 'Urban' bag uses tiny mosaics taken from selected magazine images, which are then rearranged to create a tessellated effect ■

country
Switzerland
designer
Sonja Trachsel
client
Sonja Trachsel
printer/finisher
Sonja Trachsel Villé
materials
recycled magazine pages
canvas fabric

These decorative badges are
covered with a range of
preprinted papers. Here, the
patterns are taken from the
inside of airmail envelopes and
maps of various kinds ■

country
UK
designer
Mark Pawson
client
Mark Pawson
materials
**airmail envelopes
maps**

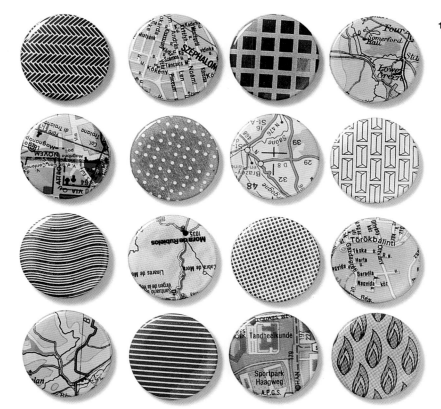

132 Made from a material akin to paper, this extraordinary head dress was one of a collection of garments created for a dance company. The combination of lightness and crispness of form, which would not be achievable in fabric, lends itself to the movement of dance.

country
UK
designer
Kei Ito
client
**Yolande Snaith
Theatre Dance**
material
non-woven polyester

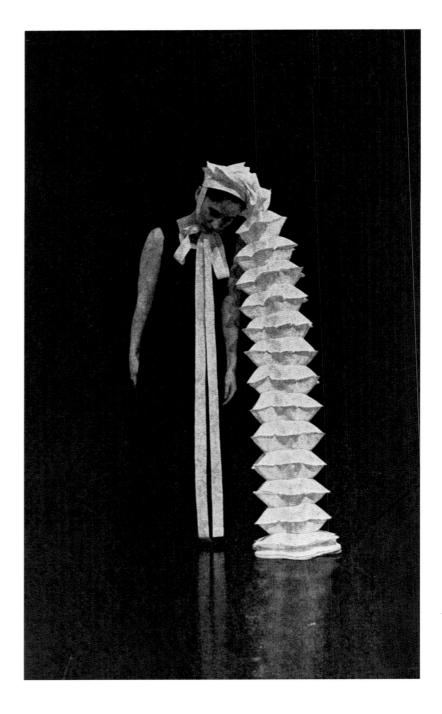

more paperwork packaging

Sunshine in a bottle is illustrated here in such a simple way. The sun, having risen by means of die-cutting, appears to have vacated a hole through which the wine can be seen.

country
UK
design practice
Kysen
client
Vignerons Catalans
stock
Centaure 80gsm

136 Originally intended to carry Dutch tulip bulbs, these recycled brown paper bags also work perfectly for the packaging for 'howies: 100% organic T-shirts', and reflect the environmental ethics of the company. The mesh-covered aperture, there to ventilate the bulbs, makes a perfect window for viewing the garment inside ■

country
UK
design practice
Carter Wong Tomlin
client
howies
printer
Fiorini International, Italy
stock
**recycled brown paper
bulb bag**

138 This elegant and restrained identity, for a company offering a select corporate gift service, uses the same device for everything from the letterhead to the luxury gift packaging. Each item is literally wrapped with a paper band that neatly locks into itself, by means of a series of folds and die-cuts. The subdued colours and the blind embossing add to the feeling of quality that this packaging exudes.

country
UK
design practice
Pentagram, London
designers
Hazel MacMillan
Laura Coley
art director
John McConnell
client
Langford & Co
printer
Fernedge
manufacturer
box: M&M Bell
stock
band: Canson Ingre

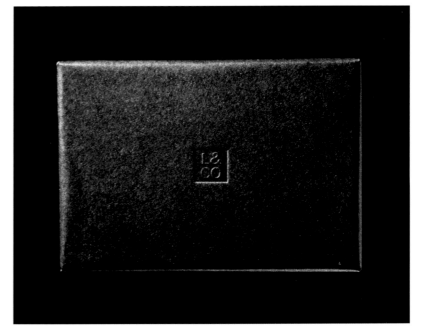

140 Only one quarter of a flower is printed in the bottom of this beautifully constructed gift box. It appears whole, as the sides are lined with mirrored paper. The intrigue is further enhanced by the black rose stems that are printed onto the silver.

country
Japan
design practice
Draft
designer
Yoshie Watanabe
client
Vitras
printer
Pastel Company
manufacturer
box: Kinko Package Company
stock
Milt Ga 105gsm
Ga Bagasse Soft 105gsm

Designed for a Japanese mail-order company, this colourful, reversible packaging is a great way to keep the customers entertained. There's the promise of what's to come when the stripes are on the outside and a lovely surprise when they're on the inside. Further variations were achieved by changing the colour palette, thereby balancing the cost of the expensive gravure plates ■

country
Japan
design practice
Sayuri Studio
designers
Sayuri Shoji
Yoshiko Shimizu
client
Felissimo Corporation
stock
craft corrugated carton

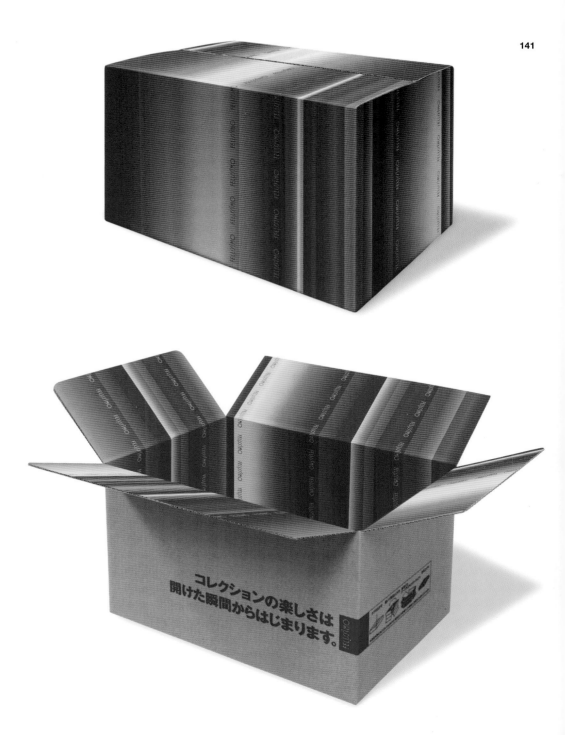

142 A combination of beautiful
paper, antique style ribbon and
laser cutting were used to
create the look of this packaging
for a top fashion designer,
synonymous with her approach,
which mixes vintage detail with
cutting edge design. The laser-
cut logo has an appropriate
star-like quality and even pierces
the ribbon.

country
UK
design practice
The Partners
designers
Greg Quinton
Jack Renwick
client
Stella McCartney

These beautifully delicate
origami boxes were created to
contain the sugared almonds
presented to guests at weddings.
Folded from greaseproof paper,
a series of unique designs
has been created, some of which
appear to burst into flower.

country
Italy
designer
Sachiko Mizoguchi
client
Dovetusai
manufacturer
Sachiko Mizoguchi
stock
greaseproof paper

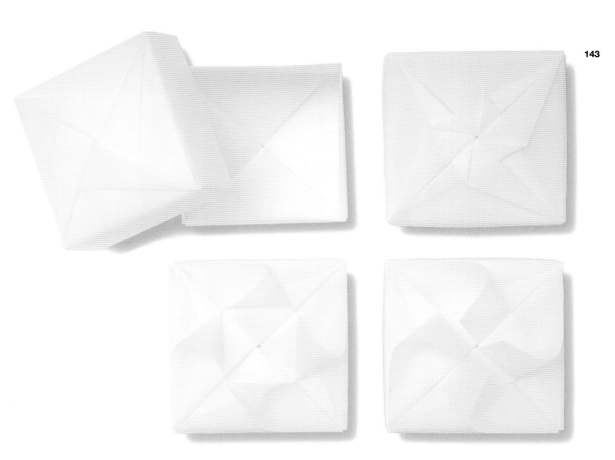

144 More like a work of art, this,
believe it or not, is the
packaging for a box set of CDs
for 'Sampled Life', an opera by
Ryuichi Sakamoto.
It reflects the work of this
avant-garde composer, using a
series of books in varying
sizes, bound in different ways,
printed in a wealth of whites,
varnishes, blacks and greys.
The subtle but complex
way in which the information
inside is presented encourages
the reader to become involved,
to delve, interpret and draw
their own conclusions about
the work.

country
Japan
design practice
Nakajima Design
designer
Hideki Nakajima
art directors
Hideki Nakajima
Norika Sky Sora
client
Warner Music Japan
printer/finisher
Agle
stock
cast-coated paper
matt-coated art
satin-coated art
uncoated Japanese paper

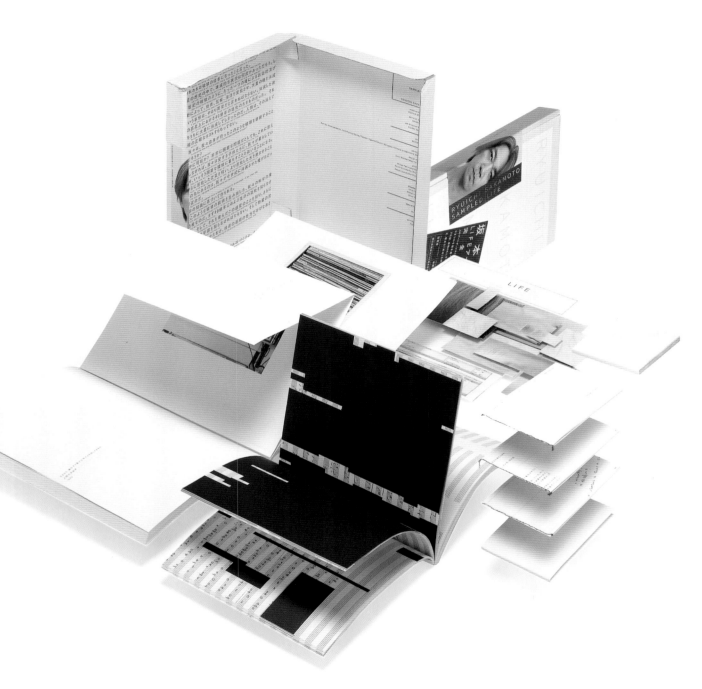

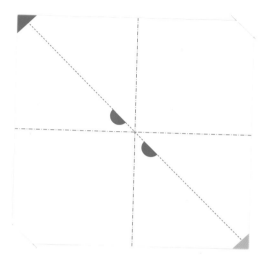

146 **Bookmark** Remove the attached pattern. Crease the diagonal line, keeping symbols on the outside. Open, then make remaining creases with symbols on inside. Encourage diagonal fold to meet in the centre. Holding all triangles together, fold down and tuck inside to meet dot. When not in use, store book mark on right-angled slot.

Made from recycled newsprint
and yellow pages, this 'pet pod'
uses layers of papier mâché
to form a vented dome that
is warm and comfortable for the
pet – the cat in the photograph
didn't want to get out – while
being aesthetically pleasing in
shape and texture ■

country
UK
design practice
Andrew Vaccari
designer
Andrew Vaccari
manufacturer
Andrew Vaccari
material
**paper pulp made from
newsprint and yellow pages**

148 Amusingly entitled 'time travel', the case of this cardboard clock doubles as the means of posting and is personalized automatically for the recipient, when addressed. The clock comes complete with an integral support strut ∎

country
UK
design practices
Northwards
Draught Associates
designers
Chris Jackson
Paul Stafford
client
2pm Limited
manufacturer
2pm Limited
printer/finisher
Colour Graphics
materials
E flute board craft 150gsm
test brown 150gsm

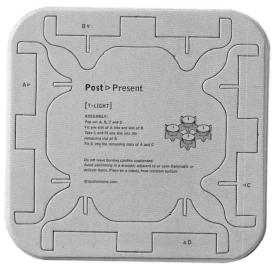

Transforming the flat into the third dimension is this designer's forte. The 'post present' (left) uses a pre-cut card that is sent out flat, for the recipient to make into this candle holder. Meanwhile the offcuts from the centre of two coat hangers (right) lock cleverly together to make a pencil rack ■

country
UK
design practice
Studiomama
designer
Nina Tolstrup
client
Studiomama
manufacturer
Allingham Hansen, Denmark
materials
coat hanger: greyboard 3mm
candle holder: greyboard 2mm

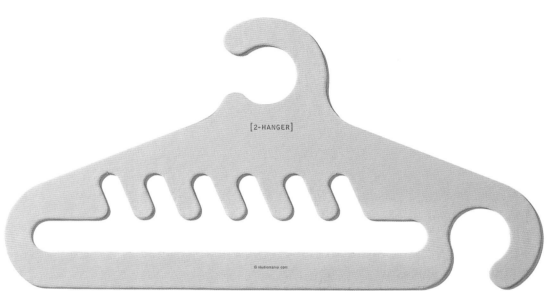

150

Recycling at its best, with no nasty chemical processes involved, these 'paperbags' are made directly from unused billboard posters, which are sewn together. The surface design of each bag varies, depending on which poster it is from ■

country
Netherlands
designer
Jos van der Meulen
client
Goods
material
recycled billboard posters

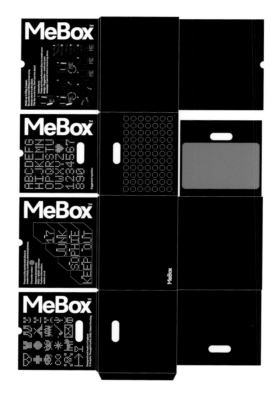

The beauty of this storage system is its versatility. The double-skinned boxes, made from one sheet of corrugated board, are pre-cut with a matrix of circles. When punched out, they reveal the contrasting colour beneath and can be used to either label or decorate the box. In this case they have been piled high to carry a much bigger message for an exhibition ■

country
UK
design practice
Graphic Thought Facility
client
Graphic Thought Facility
material
corrugated board

As well as stunning paper
buildings, this architect
also designs elegant furniture,
such as 'Carta', a range made
entirely from cardboard and
fine paper tubes ■

country
Japan
design practice
Shigeru Ban Architects
designer
Shigeru Ban
manufacturer
Cappellini
materials
cardboard tubes
cardboard

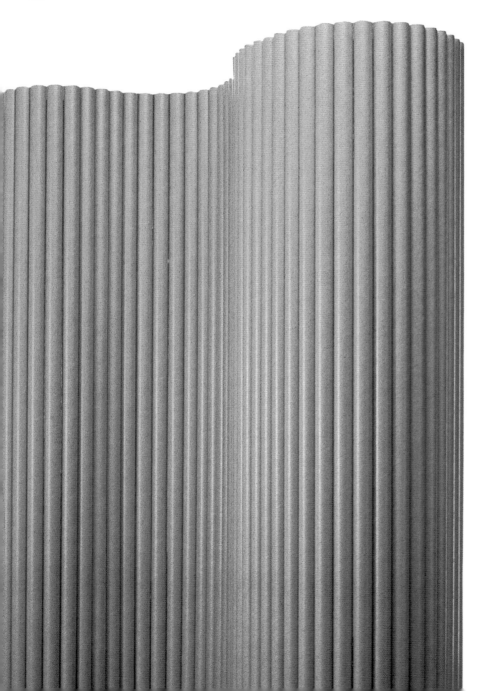

In this witty 'post it lamp' the
packaging and the product are
one. The tube, which can be
personalized, contains all that is
needed to make a light, including
a specially designed paper
clip that fits around the lamp
fitting and holds the shade ■

country
UK
design practice
2pm Limited
designer
Stewart Robbins
client
2pm Limited
manufacturer
2pm Limited
materials
card tube
plastic end caps
strip of parchment
electrical assembly
light bulb
paper clip
end stickers
instruction sheet

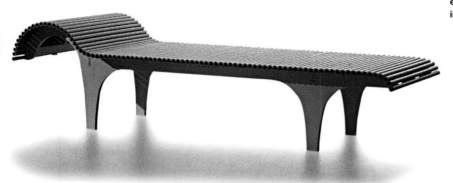

154 Designed for children and young
people on the move, this range
of furniture uses nearly all
the properties of paper. Die-cut,
folded and locked into place,
using innovative joints to create
shape and strength, the pieces
can be used unadorned as they
are, or decorated by the owner.
The nest of tables won an
American International Design
Resource Award ■

country
Croatia
design practice
Ksenija Jurinec
client
Ksenija Jurinec
material
corrugated board

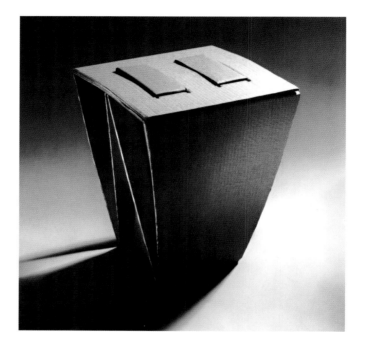

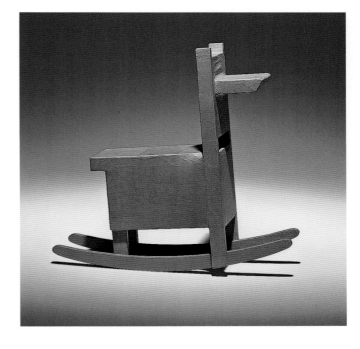

Although the frame of this characterful rocking horse is wooden, the surface is made up from several layers of brown paper, chosen for its warmth and comfort. These have been coated to create a spongeable surface, upon which children enjoy drumming.

country
Switzerland
designer
Robert A Wettstein
client
Robert A Wettstein
materials
craft paper
wooden frame

Inspired by workers in Sào Paulo, who gather discarded boxes for a living, these designers wanted to see how they could utilize such material. This multi-layered approach gives the objects great strength, while the nature of the fluted board allows light to be transmitted ■

country
Brazil
design practice
Campana Objetos
designers
Fernando and
Humberto Campana
client
Campana Objetos
materials
corrugated cardboard 3mm
aluminium frame

The work of this designer (left) is magical, as is reflected in the name 'Midsummer Light'. Whereas a lot of paper furniture gives the impression of weight, his designs are as delicate as could be and, when layered, the effect of the intricate, die-cut patterns is quite mesmerizing.

country
UK
designer
Tord Boontje
manufacturer
Artecnica
material
Tyvek®

Fascinated by geometry and the idea of designing around found objects, the designer of this 'Espresso Light' (right) was, not surprisingly, inspired by a paper coffee cup. In all, forty-two cups and twelve daisy-like gaskets interlock, without glue, to create this striking light – or any number of other objects. Continuing the spirit of recycling, suggested uses for the offcuts are made. Another light in the same collection features paper soup lids. Both lights appear at 'Coffee@' Internet cafes ■

country
UK
designer
Lothair Hamann
materials
paper espresso cup
white card

158 This range of 'MaMo Nouchies' lights is inspired by all things Japanese – the name is a composite of the designers' names and that of Isamu Noguchi, to whom this collection pays homage. Maurer worked with Mombach, who developed a new technique in which he transformed the paper into different shapes using a series of folding and pulling treatments similar to traditional Japanese textile dyeing techniques.

country
Germany
designers
Dagmar Mombach
Ingo Maurer
manufacturer
Ingo Maurer
materials
bespoke Japanese paper
stainless steel
mirrored glass

Entitled 'Zettel'z', after the German word for 'scrap of paper', this dramatic chandelier explores the effect that paper has on the quality of light. It is adorned with pieces of paper printed with poems, messages and beautiful calligraphy, as well as many blank sheets which can be personalized. The delicate pages move with the lightest breeze, in stark contrast to the ridged metal branches and modified paper clips that hold them in place.

country
Germany
designer
Ingo Maurer
manufacturer
Ingo Maurer
materials
Japanese paper
stainless steel
heat-resistant frosted glass

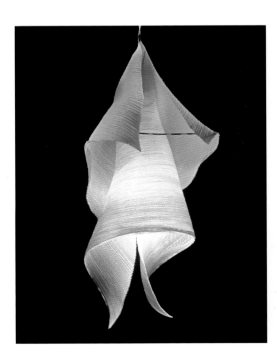

160 Adopting traditional techniques, conventionally used for making throwaway decorations, this luminous chair is delicate yet deceptively strong. Cut from a gigantic slab of honeycomb-structured paper, the contours of the chair are formed by the sitter, creating a sensual and organic shape.

country
Japan
design practice
Tokujin Yoshioka Design
designer
Tokujin Yoshioka
client
Tokujin Yoshioka
manufacturer
Tokujin Yoshioka
material
honeycomb tissue paper

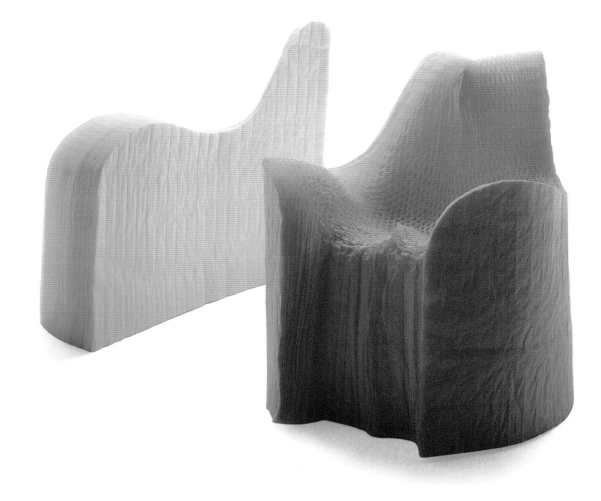

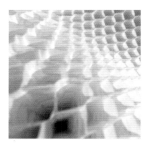

This section comprises a comprehensive list of terms and techniques that are either directly or indirectly related to paper. Entries are listed alphabetically and cross referenced where appropriate. As there are so many binding references, they have been listed together under **bookbinding terms**. The same applies to **Japanese paper terms**.

'A' series International ISO range of paper sizes, reducing from the largest (AO is 841 x 1189mm), by folding in half to preserve the same proportions at each reduction. See **sizes of paper**

abaca Plant more commonly known as Manilla hemp. See **hemp**

abrasiveness The property of the paper surface.

absorbency The degree to which paper takes up moisture.

acid free Free from acid-producing chemicals. Of more concern to fine artists than designers, acid-free papers are more durable and less prone to yellowing than others.

airbrush Pen-shaped tool that sprays a fine mist of ink or paint.

air dried Paper dried by a current of warm air after tub sizing.

airmail Extremely lightweight paper, usually below 40gsm, used for stationery and book interleaves. See **onion skin**

all-rag paper Paper created from a pulp made of rags. Now also refers to paper made of cotton-linter pulp.

antique A printing paper with a rough finish but good printing surface, valued in book printing for its high volume. Available in laid or woven.

aqueous coating Water-based coating applied like ink by a printing press to protect and enhance the printing beneath.

archival paper A paper with long-lasting qualities, not only acid-free but also lignin- and sulphur-free, most commonly used to repair historic documents.

artists' original High-quality paper, often made from a rag or cotton furnish, that simulates handmade paper but is made in a continuous process using a cylinder-mould machine.

art paper and board Highly calendered china clay or chalk-coated papers. See **gloss-art papers**

'B' series International ISO range of sizes designated for large items (wall charts and posters) and falling between 'A' series sizes: BO is 1,000 x 1,414mm. See **sizes of paper**

back Marks left in a sheet of handmade paper where it has been dried over ropes.

backing up Printing the reverse side of a sheet already printed.

bamboo Now rarely used in the production of paper, its fibres are short and needle shaped.

bank Lightweight wood-free writing and printing paper, 45–60gsm, available in tints for correspondence and copy typing in multi-part sets. See **NCR**

banker Style of envelope with an opening on the long edge and diamond shape flap. Described as either high cut or low cut depending upon the throat.

base page When referring to a pop-up, the page to which the pop-up is attached.

base paper Paper before coating, also called body paper and body stock.

basic size Standard paper size used to calculate basis weight in the USA and Canada.

basis weight The weight of paper in grams per square metre, in the USA and Canada.

basket felt Paper with a weave-effect finish, used for heavy Manilla papers.

batik Technique using wax before dyeing, so that the treated area does not pick up colour.

bible paper A very thin opaque paper for airmail, bibles, diaries, reference books, etc.

binding The joining of leafs or signatures together with either wire, glue or other means. See **bookbinding terms**

blade coated Refers to the steel blade that levels and controls the china clay coating applied to base paper. See **gloss-art** and **matt-coated papers**

162 **bleached mechanical** Paper made of chemically bleached mechanical pulp, sometimes called improved newsprint. Used for inexpensive, one- or two-colour magazines.
bleed Additional margin allowed for pictures that spread into the trim area.
blind embossing Embossing without using ink to create a raised design in paper or card that is visible because of the shadow it casts; very dark stocks lessen the shadow effect. It is not suitable for items that need to be be photocopied, faxed or laser printed.
blind image Image debossed, embossed or stamped, but not printed with ink.
See **blind embossing**
blistering Heavy-coated stocks can blister if printed by heat-set web offset. The heat used to dry the ink causes the moisture in the paper to form blisters.
block In fashion, the cardboard master from which the patterns are taken.
blotting Highly absorbent paper used for soaking up excess liquids, for example, ink.
blow up An enlargement, usually used in relation to graphic images or photographs.
board Term for paper above 220gsm, includes many grades, multi-ply, coated and uncoated.
body paper Paper before coating, also called base paper and body stock.
bookbinding terms:
adhesive binding Single sheets glued together along the spine. Also called 'unsewn binding'.
back Spine of a book, along which the leaves or sections are fastened. Also called 'backbone'.
back fold The inner margin of a folded section, where the sections are secured by stitching. Also called 'binding margin'.
back matter The back pages of a book containing references, appendices etc.
bands The cords or thongs on which the sections of the book are sewn. Recessed bands lie flat or slightly below the surface of the backbone. Raised bands are not recessed but form ridges along the backbone.
bead The top edge of a book when viewing the book upright. Also refers to the little roll formed by the knot of an endband.
blanket stitch A method of sewing in which the thread passes from one side of the section to the other and is then interlaced with the loop created on the reverse.
blind folio A page number not printed on the page; a blank page does not traditionally have a page number. See *folio*
blurb A description or commentary of an author or book content, on the book jacket.
bolt The folds that occur at the head and foredge when a sheet is folded into a section.
book block Folded signatures gathered, sewn and trimmed, but not yet covered.
book board Used to form the foundation of book covers, usually covered with either cloth, leather, paper or other materials. Also called 'binders board'.
bookcloth Book covering material made from woven cotton. See *buckram*
book jacket General term applied to printed dust cover or wrapper on books.
buckram Strong and expensive book covering made from woven linen or a mixture of linen and cotton.
burst perfect bind To bind by forcing glue into notches along the spine of gathered signatures before affixing a paper cover. Also called 'burst bind', 'notch bind' and 'slotted bind'.
case When the front and back boards, together with the covering material to which they are stuck, form a cover for the sewn sections (often associated with edition binding).
case binding A mass-produced, machine-bound book, with a case rather than a cover. Also called 'edition binding'.
comb binding To bind by inserting the teeth of a flexible comb through holes punched along the edge of a stack of paper. See *loose-leaf binding*
core Cord or rolled material, generally leather, that forms a cylindrical support. The endband is formed on a core.
cross over Type or artwork that continues from one page of a book or magazine across the gutter to the opposite page. Also called 'bridge', 'gutter bleed' and 'gutter jump'.

cut flush Describes a binding in which the cover is the same size as the sections.
dentelle An outer border on the inside or outside of a cover comprising small-tooled motifs resembling lace or 'teeth'.
doublure Material pasted onto the inside of the cover board, separate from the flyleaf. Leather, vellum or silk may be used as well as paper.
endbands Collective term used to describe headbands and tailbands.
endpaper Strong paper used for securing the body of a book to its case.
filling in To fill in the space on the inside of the front or back board left uncovered by the cloth or covering material. This creates a level surface so that the endpapers lie flat.
finishing The second of two principles involved in bookbinding includes the decoration and polishing of the cover. See *forwarding*
flush binding Binding when the cover is the same size as the sections. Also called 'cut flush'.
fly leaf A blank page at the beginning or end of a book.
fold-out A typical fold-out opens to an extra page beyond the foredge of the book and offers the opportunity for an illustration or image that is wider than a two-page spread, there can be fold-ups or fold-downs as well as fold-outs. They are added by sewing in a single sheet between any two sheets, though an entire book may consist of compiled fold-outs.
folio In book production, a sheet of paper that is folded to form pages, always comprising multiples of four. Also refers to page numbers. See *signature*
foredge The front edge of the book opposite the spine.
forwarding The first of the two principal processes involved in bookbinding includes folding, rounding, backing, headbanding and reinforcing. See *finishing*
French fold Term used to describe concertina-folded pages which are bound at the spine, creating looped pages.
French groove In the library style, the groove between the edge of the spine and the board. Its function is to enable the thick leather used in this style of binding to fold easily at the hinge.
French sewing Sewing together one or more sections without tape, done by catching the loop of thread from the previous section.
frontispiece An illustration facing the title page of a book.
gate fold Describes pages which fold inward from a central page.
gathering Collecting the sections together in the correct sequence to make a book.
gauffering Decorating the edges of a (usually gilded) book by using heated finishing tools or rolls which indent small repeat patterns.
guard book A type of binding where the spine is bulked out so it is the right depth when inserts are added, using narrow strips or folds of paper, as in photograph albums.
guards Strips of paper or cloth pasted or glued onto the back folds of sections, or onto single diagrams or maps, for their repair and reinforcement. The term can also apply to the narrow folds or strips of paper or card used in guard books. Also called 'guarding'.
gutter The blank space or printed area between pages that runs into the margin.
half bound Where the spine and corners, or spine and foredge, are covered in a good material, often leather, and a cheaper one is used to cover the remainder.
half title The recto of the first or second leaf of the book, on which the title is printed.
head Top edge of a binding or page.
headband A headband consists of coloured threads entwined tightly around a core of vellum, backed with leather, which is sewn through the sections filling in the gap at the spine, to help lessen the damage done when the book is pulled from the shelf by its headcap. Sometimes, for purely decorative reasons, an imitation headband is stuck to the back folds of the sections.
headcap In leather bindings, a shaped turn-in over the top and bottom of the spine.
hinged cover Perfect bound cover scored 3mm from the spine so that it folds at the hinge to avoid stress on the spine.

hinges The sections of a cover adjoining the spine that are glued to the book block in the binding process.

imposition Method of arranging the pages of a book so that they are in the correct sequence when the sheet is printed and folded.

inner joint The inside hinge of the cover made by the fold of the endpapers.

inset Item inserted into a book, fixed by sewing or sticking, for example, an illustration plate.

interscrew Screw and threaded tube used to bind loose-leafed items such as portfolios – can be made of metal or plastic.

ISBN International Standard Book Number. The number assigned to a published work.

Japanese stab binding There are four traditional Japanese stab bindings: Asa-No-Ha Toji – hemp leaf binding, Koki Toji – noble binding, Kikko Toji – tortoise-shell binding and Yotsume Toji – Japanese four-hole binding. The noble binding is also referred to as Kangxi binding.

kettle stitch A stitch or knot made at the end of a section to join it to the preceding one. (From the German word, ketteln, 'to pick up stitches'.) Also called 'catch stitch'.

knock up To tap sections or sheets at the spine and head so they lie squarely. Also called 'jog'.

lay flat binding Method of perfect binding that allows a book to lie flat when open.

leaf One sheet of paper in a book; each side of the leaf is one page.

library style A utility binding, it has strength and durability due to sewn-on tapes, reinforced endpapers and a thick leather cover. Its main feature is the French groove.

limp binding A soft cover, very often with both squares extending over half the thickness of the book, enclosing the edges of the pages. Bibles are often limp bound. See **squares**

linings Pieces of strong paper pasted onto the inside of boards to prevent them being warped by the covering material. Alternatively, the two pieces of material that are used to strengthen the spine, the first being of mull, the second being kraft.

loose-leaf binding Made up of single sheets of paper that are loosely held together by thongs, cords, rings, wire spirals, plastic combs, bars or spring mechanisms. Also called 'mechanical binding'.

mull Loosely woven cotton fabric used for lining the spine of books. Also called 'crash'.

nested Signatures assembled inside one another in the proper sequence for binding, as opposed to gathered.

overcasting Reinforcing a section, or joining single sheets together, by sewing through the back margin. Often used to reinforce first and last sections. Also called 'oversewing'.

pagination Numbering of the pages.

perfect binding Sections of a book are milled off along the bolt, then notched and glued together before drawing on the cover. Pages cannot be opened out flat and can only be used satisfactorily on spines more than 3mm thick.

plates Diagrams and illustrations printed on different paper from the text, and bound either with the text or tipped in as separate leaves or sections.

prelims The preliminary pages of a book, comprising the half-title page, the frontispiece, the title page, the imprint page, the contents page and any other pages up to the beginning of the main text. Prelims often form the first section. In older books, these pages are usually numbered with Roman numerals. Also called 'preliminaries' and 'preliminary matter'.

quarter bound Where the spine is covered in a good material, extending over part of the sides as well, and a cheaper one is used to cover the remainder.

recto The right-hand page of a book, usually with an odd page number.

register A page marker made of ribbon, one end glued to the spine before lining.

round back binding To case bind with a rounded, convex spine.

saddle-wire stitching Correct term for binding wire – has the appearance of staples. Available in steel or copper, can be formed into loops on the spine for use in ring binders.

self cover Cover that uses the same paper as text pages.

sewn binding A binding made up of sections sewn together.

side stitching Securing sections or a number of single sheets together by sewing with thread or inserting wire though the back margin.

signature A printed sheet of paper that, on folding, becomes a section of a book. Also refers to the sheet once folded. See **folio**

singer sewn Industrial version of domestic sewing machine stitching, used for binding. Usually stitches go through the book front but can, with skilled finishing, run from the spine through to the centre of, for example, a brochure.

spine The part of a book's jacket or cover that encloses the inner edges of the pages, facing outwards when the book is on the shelf and typically bearing the title and author's name.

squares The space between the boards or cover of a book and the sections. The size is dependent on the size, use and binding style of the book. Although the squares protect the leaves they should not be too large, for the covers must themselves be supported by the book block. Also called 'overhang'.

stab binding To secure a large number of sheets together by driving metal staples more than half way through the back margins from both sides. Also called 'stab stitching'.

stationery binding Used for binding blank leaved books intended to be written in, for example account books or ledgers.

stiff leaf Piece of paper attached by adhesive to another to increase its substance and strength – the endpaper is an example of this.

swell Additional thickness in the sewn folds of a section caused by the sewing thread and any additional repairs.

swiss binding Where cloth is glued around the spine and hinge area of the block and the cover is only glued onto the back hinge.

tail The bottom of a binding or page.

tailband Like the headband, but at the tail of the book. See **headband**

text block The sections, sewn or unsewn, that make up the text of the book.

thread sewing Signatures of a book are sewn together before binding in 8, 16 and sometimes 32. This enables pages to be opened out flat.

three-hole sewings Traditional alternative to saddle-wire stitching, using a single thread in a figure of eight.

tip in To incorporate a single sheet, plate, endpaper or section into a book using a narrow strip of adhesive. Also called 'tip on'.

title page The recto of the third or fourth leaf of a book, which carries the complete title of the book and other information such as author, publisher's name, date of publication etc.

turn over The part of the covering material that is turned over the edges of the boards to protect them. It is characteristic of all books except for some flush bindings. Also called 'turn in' and 'overlap'.

verso A left-hand page of a book, usually with an even page number.

whole binding A binding that is covered entirely in the same material. Also called 'full binding'.

wrap-around cover Describes a cover that is not physically attached to the pages beneath, but held in place by the friction caused by 'wrapping' it around them.

yapp binding Binding with squares extended to overlap the exposed edges of the paper and cover them completely. Yapp bindings are usually limp, with rounded corners, and are used mainly for devotional books such as prayer books. Also called 'limp binding'. See **squares**

bond uncoated Paper generally used as writing paper.

bonding strength The extent to which fibres at the surface of the paper adhere to one another and to the fibres below the surface.

book paper General term for paper specifically made for book production.

brittleness The extent to which paper cracks or breaks when bent or embossed.

brightness The extent to which a paper reflects white light.

164

bristol board High-quality smooth board.

broadside The term used to indicate work printed on one side of a large sheet of paper.

broke Damaged or defective paper often discarded during manufacture, usually re-pulped.

broken ream Part of a ream of paper left after use.

bronzing The effect produced by dusting wet ink after printing using a metallic powder.

brush coated Method of coating paper using oscillating brushes with a mineral substance such as china clay.

build a colour To overlap two or more screen tints to create a new colour. Also called 'build', 'tint build', 'stacked screen build' and 'colour build'.

bulk The thickness of a paper measured by calliper, volume or ppi.

bulky mechanical Paperback books, office/store cash/adding machine paper.

burst A means to gauge strength of paper.

bursting Term referring to the separation of perforated sheets.

butter paper Vegetable parchment, rather like greaseproof paper.

butt register Register where ink colours meet precisely without overlapping or allowing space between, as compared to lap register. Also called 'butt kiss' and 'kiss register'. See **lap register**

'C' series ISO envelope sizes, to fit stationery of 'A' series dimensions. See **sizes of paper**

C1S C2S Abbreviation of coated one side and coated two sides.

C roll Large cylindrical roller used on a Fourdrinier machine, which impresses the watermark onto the paper. See **Fourdrinier**

calcium/magnesium carbonate buffered The process of adding either calcium carbonate or magnesium carbonate to paper pulp to counteract the natural acidity of the woodpulp.

calender Set of rollers through which paper passes under pressure to impart a smooth finish. See **supercalender**

calendered paper High-glaze paper, polished by pressure or friction from calendering rollers.

caliper The thickness of a single sheet of paper measured in millimetres, microns or 1/1000 inch. A micron is 1/1000mm.

carbon paper Base paper usually comprising a thin tissue or other lightweight grade, coated on one side with a mixture of carbon black or other colouring agent and a chemical substance that acts as a carrier.

carbonless paper The application of pressure on the top sheet causes gelatin capsules on the reverse, containing a transparent chemical, to break. The chemical reacts with the coating on the top of the sheet below, causing the writing to appear. Also called 'self copy'.

cardboard tubes Made from layers of generally recycled paper, straight wound (convolute) or spiral wound, and glued together. Subject to individual manufacturers, available in sizes starting from 20mm diameter to in excess of 600mm, wall thickness of 1mm to more than 30mm for special orders. Lengths can be cut to whatever is required. Generally in the neutral colour of the material but can be coated in one of many finishes available. Also called 'paper tubes' and 'mailing tubes'.

cartridge paper Printing or drawing paper with good dimensional stability, high opacity and good bulk. Is prone to ink rub, but this can be prevented using inks with a high wax content. Used for drawing paper, envelopes etc.

cast coated papers High gloss, coated paper made by pressing the paper against a polished, hot, metal drum while the coating is still wet.

catalogue paper Coated paper commonly used for catalogues and magazines with a basis weight of 50 to 75gsm.

chain lines Watermark lines that run at right angles to laid lines on the laid surface of the mould.

chalking Term used in heat-set web offset when the ink does not adhere to the surface of the paper and can be removed by rubbing.

character The distinctive characteristics of a paper such as wove or laid.

chemical pulp Pulp produced by treating wood with chemicals to break down the fibres rather than grinding mechanically. It contains fewer impurities than mechanical pulp, is stronger, and produces paper which is less likely to yellow when exposed to light. Also called 'wood-free' papers. See **mechanical wood pulp**

cheque papers Chemically treated security paper, usually made to specification, which may contain watermarks and other security features against fraud.

china clay A white, refined clay used extensively in loading and coating paper surfaces.

chin colle Sheets of paper laminated together by the pressure of an etching press and glue.

chipboard A cheap grade of board usually manufactured from lower grades of waste paper and available unlined or lined on one or both sides.

chlorine compounds The chemical group used in pulp and papermaking to bleach the pulp. See **TCF** and **ECF**

chromo coated One-sided coated, high-quality gloss paper or board for proofing and inserts.

cloth lined Paper with a muslin/linen centre or backing used to strengthen. It is used for charts, maps, envelopes, identification bags, etc. Also called 'cloth centred'.

CMYK Abbreviation for cyan, magenta, yellow and key (black), the four process colours.

coated paper Paper coated with china clay or similar materials to give a smooth surface good for halftone reproduction. See **gloss-art** and **matt-coated papers**

cockling Wavy edges of paper caused by unstable atmospheric conditions.

cold pressed (CP) The slightly rough surface quality of a sheet of paper. See **not**

collage When pieces of paper, photographs or ephemera are arranged, and stuck to a background, to form an image.

collate To organize printed matter in a specific order.

colour balance Refers to the amount of process colours that simulate the colours of the original image or photograph.

concertina fold Folded literally like the bellows section of a concertina. Also called 'accordion fold' and 'accordion pleat'.

conditioning Keeping paper in controlled conditions to achieve moisture equilibrium.

conservation paper Generic term for papers used in conservation work as they are low in acidity, are dimensionally stable and have a long life expectancy.

continuous stationery Stationery paper in perforated reel, or folded, for automatic feed.

copier paper Lightweight grades of paper used in photocopying machines.

corrugated board Board made largely of recycled paper and most commonly comprises three components: an outer and inner 'liner' (the flat surface components) and a 'corrugating medium' (the fluting), which is glued between the liners. It is this sandwich type construction that gives it its rigidity and structural strength and unique cushioning characteristics. Corrugated board comes in the following sizes (typical caliper in mm):

single face corrugated board
E flute 1.1–1.8 *B flute* 2.1–3.0 *C flute* 3.2–3.9 *A flute* 4.0–4.8
single-wall corrugated board
B flute 2.95 *C flute* 3.78
double-wall corrugated board
EB flute 4.06 *BC flute* 6.50 *CC flute* 7.33

copperplate printing Traditional process carried out with a hand-engraved copper plate, which uses the intaglio method. Generally used for invitations and business cards.

cotton fibre The soft white filaments attached to the seeds of the cotton plant. Cotton fabric is made from the long fibres, leaving behind short fibres, called linters, which can be used for papermaking. Cotton rags can also be turned into pulp for papermaking. See **rag**

cover paper and boards Used for catalogues, cards, booklets, etc.

cracking Breakline occurring where sheets of paper are folded.

crêpe paper Paper which is crimped with fine pleats, enabling it to be stretched and shaped.

cross direction Across the web, at right angles to the machine direction.

crown Paper size 508 x 381mm. See **sizes of paper**

curing Allowing paper to mature before sale.

curling A curl can be caused by several factors: difference in structure or coatings from one side to the other, moving from one atmosphere to another before printing, which may effect the paper's moisture content, or contact with the process moisture during printing, for example, during offset printing.

custom making Paper made specially to client specifications.

cut-size paper Small cut sizes for office stationery use.

cylinder mould The type of papermaking machine most commonly used today in the production of mould-made papers.

debossing Like embossing but the image or mark is sunken into the page as opposed to raised. See **embossing**

deckle On a hand mould, the deckle is the removable frame that retains the pulp on the mould while the water drains through.

deckle edge The wavy, feathered edges of a sheet of handmade or mould-made paper.

density: **ink** the relative thickness of a layer of printed ink; **colour** the relative ability of colour to absorb or reflect light, or to block light passing through it; **paper** the relative tightness or looseness of fibres.

die Device for cutting, scoring, stamping, embossing and debossing.

die-cut To cut irregular shapes in paper or paperboard using a die.

die stamping Process similar to embossing that uses a female die into which the paper is pressed. In this case, the recess of the die is coated with either oil- or water-based inks. Metallic inks are sometimes polished by a second 'hit' without ink. Not recommended for laminated, varnished or cast-coated stocks. Traditionally used for crests and logos.

dimensional stability The dimensional stability of a paper is the percentage of elongation or shrinkage caused by a given change in the relative humidity or moisture content in the air. It is a measure of the paper's tendency to cause misregister.

discolouration Most papers tend to yellow as they age, particularly in a polluted atmosphere. Papers made from mechanically pulped wood will yellow much more quickly and easily than those made of chemically pulped wood (wood free). Cheap, coloured papers will fade in sunlight; more expensive ones may contain colouring agents resistant to this.

dished Stack of paper lying concave rather than flat.

dot and cross In fashion, the paper used for making patterns that is printed with a series of blue dots and crosses.

dot gain When halftones are printed, the dot on the paper will be bigger than the dot on the printing plate or screen. The amount by which it is bigger is the dot gain, and is dependent on factors such as the surface of the paper, the pressure used and the type of ink.

double bump To print a single image twice so that it has two layers of ink.

double coated Paper that has received two coatings of the same or different materials.

DPI Dot per inch – used to describe fineness of a printer's screen – usually 150–400DPI.

drawing papers and boards High-quality papers, either handmade or mould made, often tub sized and with an all-rag furnish.

Dufex A registered technique that uses specially engraved plates to emboss the surface of aluminium foil-laminated paper or cardboard, enhancing the reflective quality of the surface and adding movement and depth. This process can be used on its own – Dufex only – or to treat images printed onto the foil using transparent ink. Generally used for greetings cards, book covers and various commercial applications.

dry pressing Name for various pressing sequences applied to sheets of paper after drying.

dull finish Flat (not glossy) finish on coated paper, slightly smoother than matt. Also called 'suede finish', 'velour finish' and 'velvet finish'.

duodecimo A sheet of paper folded with a z-fold to form a section of 12 leaves or 24 pages. See **z-fold**

duplex papers and boards Lamination of two papers of different colour or quality.

duplicating papers Unsized and semi-sized papers with a built-in quick drying facility for use in the duplicating process.

dust jacket Protective outer wrapping of a book or brochure.

ECF (**Elemental Chlorine Free**) ECF pulps are made without chlorine gas.

eco label Eco labels are environmental labelling schemes run by numerous bodies in various countries. They include: ***Blue Angel*** – Germany; ***NF Environment*** – France; ***Nordic Swan*** – Norway, Sweden, Denmark, Iceland and Finland; ***Green Seal*** – USA; ***Eco-Mark*** – Japan; ***The Environmental Choice Programme***, which has been taken up by countries including Canada, New Zealand and Australia.

embossing Creating a raised surface pattern in paper or card by pressing it between a male and female metal die. For simple designs, the die can be photo engraved; more complex patterns have to be engraved by hand, which is more expensive. To prevent the paper splitting, a non-coated stock with long or random fibres should be used. If the image is sunk into the page it can be described as debossed. Embossing can be used in conjunction with a printed or foil shape. See **blind embossing**

emulsion Coating of light-sensitive chemicals on paper.

enamel paper High gloss coated on one side.

engine sized Chemicals added to paper pulp to aid ink and water resistance. See **size**

English finish Smooth finish on uncoated book paper.

engraving Printing method using a plate, also called a die, with an image cut/engraved into its surface. See **embossing**

environmentally friendly (see **recycled**) A paper may be environmentally friendly for any/all of the following reasons:
– there is a policy of replanting to replace those trees cut down to be pulped.
– no chlorine is used in the bleaching process. Bleaching pulp with chlorine results in toxic effluent. See **ECF** and **TCF**
– high straw content, therefore less wood pulp needed.
– the papermaking process is itself environmentally friendly – for instance, the mill uses as little energy as possible, and minimizes or cleans the effluent it releases into the environment.

esparto Type of grass from North Africa with good papermaking fibre properties for smoothness in writing and printing papers.

ex-merchant stock Papers obtained direct from a merchant's warehouse.

ex-mill stock Papers ordered through a merchant for delivery from mill stock.

fastness Resistance of colour to fading. Also called 'fast-colour inks'.

felt side The side of the paper in contact with the felt after forming, opposite to the wire.

fibres The basic structural material in all sheets of paper. Most papers contain wood fibres, but fibres suitable for papermaking can be extracted from cotton, linen, jute, kozo, gampi, manila and many other materials. The longer the fibres, the stronger the paper.

fillers Substances which are added to the pulp during the beating stage to fill in the pores of the fibres, producing a harder, more opaque paper surface.

166

fine papers High-quality papers.

finish A general term for the surface characteristics of papers and boards.

finishing Processes that the printed sheet goes through in order to produce the final item, for example, creasing, die-cutting, binding etc. Also, in papermaking, refers to the practices of drying, sizing and looking over sheets of paper following the papermaking.

flax Plant, the fibres from which are used in papermaking.

flexographic Printing technique using relief rubber or plastic plates in rotary-fed production, mainly used for packaging.

flocked paper Paper covered in tiny particles, originally cotton, which are statically charged to stand on end, creating a velvet-like texture.

flood To print a sheet completely with ink or varnish.

fluorescent paper Dyed or coated with fluorescent pigments activated by ultra-violet light to glow brightly.

foam-centred board Display boards for advertising, promotions, etc.

foil blocking Technique of applying a thin layer of metal or foil to the surface of paper using the combination of a metal block, heat and pressure. It is the only way to achieve a realistic metallic appearance with a smooth, reflective surface. Can also be used to provide an opaque medium when blocking light-coloured type, or shapes, onto dark stock, or flat colour onto flecked stock.

foil emboss To foil and emboss an image. Also called 'heat stamp'.

foil papers and boards Papers and boards with a metallic laminated surface, generally used for box making, labels and wrappers, especially for food.

folding boxboard White-lined boards made from a top-quality furnish, coated, impregnated or laminated with exceptional scoring and folding properties.

folding machine There are two standard types of folding machines: the 'Buckler' – paper travels through the machine, hits a deflector and begins to buckle the paper, is then caught between rollers and pulled through, creating the fold, and the 'Knife' – as the paper travels through the machine, a knife comes down at a precise moment and hits the paper, creasing it. The paper is then caught between rollers in the same way as the 'Buckler'.

fold quality Refers to the appearance of the fold.

fold strength Measured by how many times a piece of paper can be folded back and forth before breaking.

foolscap Paper size 343 x 432mm. See **sizes of paper**

forest certification Certifies that the wood used comes from a forest that is well managed according to strict environmental, social and economic standards. Two examples are PEFC (Pan European Forest Certificate) and FSC (Forest Stewardship Council).

form Old name for a mould.

formation The fibre distribution in a sheet of paper as it appears when held up to the light.

forming The action of making a sheet of paper by dipping the mould into a vat of pulp the water drains through the cover, leaving the pulp on the surface.

Fourdrinier Type of paper machine, invented by Nicholas-Louis Robert and named after the Fourdrinier brothers who financed its early development, in which paper is made at high speed in a continuous web. See **web**

foxing The discolouration of the paper of old books or prints with brown spots.

furnish The mixture of pulp and additives from which a paper is made.

galley proof Proof of letterpress type setting before being made into pages, rarely used.

ghosting When a faint image appears on a printed sheet where it was not intended, or when an image appears too light due to ink starvation. Chemical ghosting refers to the transfer of the faint image from one sheet to the back of another. Mechanical ghosting refers to a faint image appearing as a repeat of an image on the same side of the sheet.

glassine Transparent paper used for window envelopes, photo bags, interleaving books, sweet packaging, etc. It is available embossed with intricate patterns and in rich colours.

glazing The process of smoothing a paper surface, usually by running dried sheets through steel rollers or between polished zinc plates.

gloss The light reflectiveness of the surface of a paper – a shiny or lustrous appearance.

gloss-art papers These are highly calendered china-clay or chalk-coated papers, with the following properties:
– provide the highest quality reproduction in terms of detail/definition
– the ink sits on top of the paper allowing it to dry quickly
– minimal dot distortion/dot gain
– can reproduce fine screens
– inks often appear matt against the paper surface
– opacity and bulk not as good as matt paper because of calendering.

gloss ghosting Effect caused by a combination of the paper quality and the amount of ink and varnish being carried, which can cause a yellow ghosting on the white areas of the reverse side to a dense-printed image.

glue knock out An area of paper kept free of printed ink to allow for glue to bond properly.

grain The alignment of fibres in machine, or mould-made paper due to direction of water used in the manufacturing process, sometimes called 'machine direction'. 'Long grain' or 'grain' indicates that the fibres run parallel to the longest side of a sheet; 'short grain' that they run parallel to the shortest side. Handmade paper has no grain as the fibres are distributed randomly. The grain of a machine- or mould-made paper results in the following properties:
– the paper tears more easily along the grain
– it folds more easily and sharply along the grain: hence folds should be aligned along the grain
– it is stronger and stiffer across the grain
– it expands or contracts across the grain so, when printing, should run across the machine
The following are ways of assessing the grain direction in a paper:
– on packet label of the unprinted paper; in the UK the second dimension of the sheet size indicates grain direction, for example, 450 x 640mm is long grain, 640 x 450mm is short grain
– slowly tear the paper in one direction, then again at right angles: the straightest tear will be the one in the grain direction
– wet a sample of the paper: the axis of curl is in the grain direction
– for board, flex a piece in both directions: the stiffest will be at right angles to the grain.

grammage (gsm/gm²) The weight of a single one metre square sheet of a paper. Expressed in grams per square metre.

gravure Printing technique using metal cylinders etched with tiny wells, to hold ink that is drawn out under pressure, used for high quality, long runs such as magazines. See **intaglio**

greaseproof Translucent paper, with a high resistance to penetration by grease or fats, produced by prolonged heating in the pulp stage.

greyboard Board made entirely from waste paper; used in bookbinding and packaging.

gripper edge Leading edge of paper as it passes though a printing press.

gripper margin Unprintable blank edge of paper, held by the grippers which control the flow of the sheet as it passes though the printing press.

groundwood paper Newsprint and other inexpensive paper made from pulp created when wood chips are ground mechanically rather than refined chemically.

gummed papers Base papers coated on a web with water-based adhesive.

gusset pocket An envelope with expandable sides.

gsm/gm² Grams per square metre. See **grammage**

half stuff Partially broken or beaten fibres for papermaking. See **stuff**

handmade Paper made by hand.

heat sealed Paper coated with an adhesive material that is activated by applying heat.

hemp Term for the cannabis plant from which fibres are used to make paper. Also used as a generic for plant fibres. One of the oldest fibres recorded for use in papermaking.

hickeys In offset lithography, spots or imperfections in the printing due to such things as dried ink skin, paper particles, etc. Also called 'bull's eye' and 'fish eye'.

honeycomb board Building material comprising a paper honeycomb structure, laminated both sides with paper liners. Also called 'honeycomb panels' and 'cardboard honeycomb'.

hot pressed (**HP**) Handmade or mould-made paper with a smooth surface achieved by passing sheets through hot, heavy metal plates or rollers.

hot spot Printing defect in which a piece of dirt or air bubble causes incomplete contact during platemaking, leaving an area of weak ink coverage or visible dot gain.

hygroscopic Refers to paper's tendency to absorb moisture from the air.

imitation art Paper highly loaded with china clay and gloss finish to appear like coated art.

imperial Paper size 762 x 559mm. See **sizes of paper**

imposition The arrangement of pages so they will appear in proper sequence after press sheets are folded and bound.

impression In printing, refers to either ink – one press sheet passing once through a printing unit or, the speed of a press – one press sheet passing through the press.

impression cylinder Cylinder, on a press, that pushes paper against the plate or blanket, forming the image. Also called the 'impression roller'.

imprint To print new copy on a previously printed sheet, such as imprinting an employee's name on business cards. Also called 'surprint'.

inclusions Term referring to the additional, usually decorative elements added to the paper pulp, ie. petals, leaves, gold leaf, etc.

index board Strong board usually made from chemical wood pulp, having a smooth surface and being hard sized, for index cards and stationery.

India paper Very thin, high-quality, opaque rag paper often used for bibles.

ink holdout Characteristic of paper that prevents it from absorbing ink, allowing ink to dry on the surface of the paper. Also called 'holdout'.

ink-jet paper Printing paper produced specifically for use with the ink-jet printing process.

ink-jet printing Printing process using small ink particles projected onto the paper surface.

ink rub Problem caused when the ink does not adhere firmly to the surface of the paper.

in line Any process, such as printing, drying, UV varnish, that is part of a single pass through a printing machine.

insert Additional matter placed within a book or magazine without being permanently fixed.

intaglio Printing process which uses paper and pressure to draw the ink from the recesses in an engraved plate. Most common forms are gravure and engraving.

interleaves Blank sheets or pages, usually tissue, used to protect photographs or prints.

ISO sizes Formerly DIN sizes. International range of paper and envelope sizes, comprising 'A' series, 'B' series and 'C' series. See **sizes of paper**

ivory board Used for visiting cards, high-quality notices, tickets and menus.

Japanese paper terms:

chiri A Japanese term for mulberry bark, commonly used to refer to any paper with inclusion of mulberry bark.

chiyogami Craft paper, washi printed in colour using wood blocks.

danshi High-grade wrapping paper, usually crêped, used for ceremonial purposes.

gampi Its thin, glossy fibres result in translucent papers that are very tough.

gasenshi Imitation Chinese calligraphy paper.

goyoushi Official-use paper.

hakuoshi Paper in which pieces of gold or silver leaf are pasted.

hansetushi Calligraphy and drawing paper.

hanshi Thin, light, durable and inexpensive paper used for calligraphy and accounts.

hogogami Eighth-century term for recycling.

hosho(shi) High-grade mulberry paper used for woodblock printing.

ikkanbari Paper used to create objects such as boxes and tableware; the original technique was equivalent to papier mâché.

kairyo Wood pulp version of hanshi.

kamiko Paper for clothing made by laminating washi and then crumpling to soften. It is sometimes waterproofed with oil or tannin.

kammi-nagato Items made with woven threads of shredded washi, which is then lacquered.

kankoshi 'Paper recalling the lost soul' made from the recycled letters of the dead authors.

karakami Known as 'Chinese paper', as it was first imported from northern China. Paper used for sliding screens, clothing and waterproof raincoats.

kirigami Craft using 'cut paper' as opposed to the 'folded paper' of origami.

kirihaku Paper made with the inclusion of squares of gold or silver leaf.

kozo Type of mulberry, the long, strong fibres from which paper is made.

kyokushi Smooth, thick mitsumata paper with good print surface.

mino(gami) Mulberry paper now used for stationery and books.

mitsumata Plant with long, strong fibres from which paper is made.

moroshifu Fine shreds of washi are twisted into threads and woven into fabric – shifu.

mozo Wood pulp version of hanshi.

nakaori(gami) Danshi or hososhi cut lengthwise.

noge Paper made with the inclusion of fine strips of gold or silver leaf.

okuragami Official storage paper.

origami The art of folded paper. Comes from the Japanese 'ori' *fold* and 'kami' *paper*.

ryoshi Writing paper.

shifu Woven paper clothing.

shojigami Paper used to make the sliding doors in traditional Japanese houses.

shukushi 'Water-clouded' paper – recycled paper made from printed paper waste.

su A flexible bamboo or reed screen used in Japanese papermaking.

sugihara(shi) Mulberry paper traditionally used as a gift by samurai and priests.

suki moyo Term referring to paper that is ornamented during the papermaking process.

suminagashi Japanese equivalent of marbled paper.

sunagofuri Paper made with the inclusion of small particles of gold or silver.

takeya shibori Imitation leather papers used for making purses and harnesses.

tengiyo Extremely thin mulberry paper made using a very sophisticated process, originally used by artists, now used for wrapping gems and pieces of fine art.

tobikumo Paper made with the inclusion of indigo and violet dyed fibres that is shaken to create a cloud-like effect across the sheet.

torinoko 'Child of the bird'. The name was probably given because the yellowish colour of the unbleached paper resembles that of an egg. This gampi paper is used for stationery and cards, art printing, sliding panels and semi-official documents.

uchikumo Paper made as tobikumo, but with cloud-like effect around the edge.

unryu Meaning 'Cloud dragon paper', unryu is characteristic of paper containing strands of fibre that have been added to create contrast and texture.

usuzumigami 'Slightly inked paper' – recycled paper made from printed paper waste.

washi Literally translated as 'wa', Japanese, 'shi', paper.

yookanshi Imitation leather papers used for making purses and harnesses.

yoshino Specialized paper for lacquer filtration.

168

khadi Cotton fibre from which Indian paper is made.

kiss cut To die-cut the top layer, but not the backing layer, of self-adhesive paper. Also called 'kiss die-cut' and 'face cut'.

kraft Matt and glazed Manilla paper used for wrapping purposes, which has a high mechanical strength. Also produced in white, called 'bleached kraft'.

kraft pulp (**sulphate pulp**) Any pulp made by the sulphate process, mainly a mixture of sodium hydroxide and sodium sulphide.

label paper Wide range of paper grades coated on one side with adhesive.

laid paper Paper that is made on a laid mould (as opposed to a wove mould). If laid paper is held up to the light, closely spaced parallel lines can be seen. It is customary for these laid lines to run across the page width and the chain lines from head to foot.

lamination Bonding two sheets, either of the same or differing materials, to stiffen or protect, for example, paper to board, board to matt/gloss coating.

landscape Orientation in which width is greater than height.

lap register Register where ink colours overlap slightly. See **butt register**

laser bond Bond paper made especially smooth and dry to run well through laser printers.

laser cutting A paper cutting technique whereby laser technology is utilized to cut away certain unmasked areas of paper. The cutting is the result of the exposure of the paper to the laser ray, which actually evaporates the paper. Also called 'laser engraving'.

laser imprintable ink Ink that will not fade or blister as the paper on which it is printed is used in a laser printer.

laser printing Xerographic printing in which a modulated laser ray is projected onto a photoconductive cylinder or belt by a rotating mirror. The laser serves to produce the electrostatic latent image, which is developed with toners.

lay Orientation of a sheet of paper through the printing press.

laydown Indication of the position of an artwork on a sheet of paper.

lay edge The edge of a sheet of paper feeding into a press.

leaf One sheet of paper in a book; each side of the leaf is one page.

ledger paper Strong, smooth bond paper used for keeping business records. Also called 'record paper'.

lens tissue Strong but extremely light tissue, intended for protecting lenses. Can be used for interleaving and wrapping.

lenticular Constructed from interlaced images filtered through a special plastic sheet with lens-shaped ridges on the surface. This allows differing images to be viewed, depending on the angle at which the surface is held and gives the impression of movement.

letter fold Two folds creating three panels that allow a sheet of letterhead to fit inside a business envelope. Also called 'barrel fold' and 'wrap-around fold'.

letterpress A relief form of printing, which takes the impression from an inked block or typeset metal, using pressure.

lightweight paper Papers having a grammage (basis weight) normally less than 40gsm.

lignin Substance in trees that holds cellulose fibres together.

linen Has long fibres, used to produce strong, fine papers for high-quality stationery paper.

linen finish Embossed finish on text paper that simulates the pattern of linen cloth.

linters Short cotton fibres left over from the fabric-making process. See **cotton fibre**

litho Abbreviation of offset lithographic printing. See **offset litho**

litress A smooth cartridge paper made in two sizes, Royal and Foolscap, used for drawing.

loading To mix minerals in with the pulp, for example, smalts to make it appear whiter or china clay to bulk up the fibres and act as an aid to ink retention.

long grain The fibres that run parallel to the longest side of a sheet of paper. See **grain**

m weight Term used in the US for the weight of 1,000 sheets of any given paper size.

machine coated Coating applied to base paper while on papermaking machine.

machine direction Alignment of fibres due to water direction in manufacturing. See **grain**

machine glazed Gloss finish on one side achieved by drying on large, heated cylinder.

machine made Paper that is produced on a rapidly moving machine which forms, dries, sizes and presses the sheets.

make ready All activities required to prepare a press or other machine to function for a specific printing or bindery job, as compared to production run. Also called 'set up'. Also refers to paper used in the make ready process at any stage of production – make ready paper is part of waste or spoilage.

making order Minimum quantity for special making of paper.

male die Die that applies pressure during embossing or debossing. Also called 'force card'.

manifold paper Lightweight bank paper, less than 44gsm.

Manilla paper Strong paper for envelopes and files, formerly made from hemp. When oiled it is used for making stencils.

matt-coated papers Papers with a matt coating of china clay or chalk, 12–22gsm. Properties of matt-coated papers:
– good opacity and bulk
– better durability than art papers
– the non-reflective surface enhances legibility of type
– good for high-resolution images
– will take gloss varnish
– prone to ink rub because of unevenness of surface
– the porous surface sometimes absorbs ink unevenly.
Matt-uncoated papers, from chemically processed wood pulp, have the following properties:
– high opacity and bulk
– more durable than coated papers
– do not crack along fold lines
– can have problems with set off/ink rub
– slight dot gain because of absorbency
– colours look flatter than on coated stock
– do not take varnish well
– sometimes require opaque inks
– take embossing and watermarks well
– maximum screen commonly used is 150 DPI
– good for reproducing illustrations.

mechanical wood pulp Pulp produced mechanically, by grinding the wood, rather than treating it with chemicals – also used to describe paper made of this pulp. Mechanical pulp is weaker than chemical pulp, resulting in paper that is more likely to yellow if exposed to light. Makes cheap, opaque papers used for newspaper, paperback books, etc.

metallic ink Ink containing powdered metal or pigments that simulate metal.

metallic paper Paper coated with a thin film or pigment to simulate metal.

MF Machine-finished, smooth surface obtained by on-machine calendering.

millpack A term used for 100–125 sheets of paper. See **volume/quantity of paper**

moiré Undesirable pattern resulting from halftones and screen tints being made with improperly aligned screens. Also occurs when a pattern in a photo, such as a plaid, interfaces with a halftone dot pattern.

moisture content Moisture in paper, expressed as a percentage of weight.

mottle Spotty, uneven ink absorption. Also called 'sinkage'. May also be called 'mealy'.

mould A rectangular wooden frame covered with either a laid or wove-wire surface used for forming sheets of paper by hand.

mould made Paper made on cylinder-mould machine, imitating handmade.

NAPM National Association of Paper Merchants.

NCR No carbon required. See **carbonless paper**

newsprint The cheapest printing paper, used to make newspapers. It has good opacity and bulk, but a poor surface and low brightness. Entirely made of mechanical pulp, it discolours easily. Unsuitable for screens finer than 100DPI.

Newton's rings Rainbow pattern caused when poor contact, in the scanning or film-making process, allows light to be refacted.

nonimpact printing Printing using lasers, ions, ink jets or heat to transfer images to paper.

not Slightly rough, unglazed surface of a paper (abbreviation of 'not hot pressed'). Produced when a handmade or mould-made paper is repressed without felts. This gives a surface finish between rough and hot pressed.

OCR paper High-quality, wood-free bond for optical character recognition.

octavo A sheet of paper that is folded in half on the long side three times to make a section of eight leaves or 16 pages.

offset litho printing Offsets the right reading image from a flat, sensitized plate on to a blanket cylinder before transferring to the paper. This process uses the property of oil on water not mixing. See **sheet fed** and **web printing**

one-sided art High-quality paper coated on one side for book jacket covers.

onion skin Extremely lightweight paper with a cockle finish. See **air mail**

opacity The extent to which printing on the reverse of a sheet of paper shows through; the more opaque the paper is, the less likely it is that the printing will show through.

optical brightener Dye used to brighten paper by fluorescence to UV.

out of the page Any part of a pop-up that is die-cut directly from the base page.

ozalid proof Dye line print taken from film before printing plates are made. Used as cheap alternative to printed proofs or to check the right corrections have been made.

PAA Paper Agents Association.

painted sheet Sheet printed with ink edge to edge, as compared to spot colour. The painted sheet refers to the final product, not the press sheet, and means that 100 percent coverage results from bleeds off all four sides.

pallet Wood base, holding specific quantity of paper.

pantone A system for matching colours, used in specifying printing inks.

papier mâché French for 'chewed paper', it is a mixture of paper and glue that can be formed into any shape. Its inherent strength and lightness makes it ideal for packaging.

papyrus Material made of sliced sections of the inner pithy body of the flower stem of the papyrus plant, laid in two layers at right angels, pressed and dried together, mainly associated with Ancient Egypt. The name 'paper' is derived from the word 'papyrus'.

parchment Sheep or goatskin (with the hair removed) that has been split, soaked, limed and dried under tension, not tanned like leather.

parent sheet Any sheet larger than A3.

particle gummed paper Base paper coated with remoisturable adhesive in small particles to ensure paper remains flat.

part mechanical Paper containing up to 50 percent of mechanical pulp.

paste board Used for high-quality heavyweight boxes for cosmetics and confectionery.

perfecting The technical term for printing the second or reverse side of a sheet.

perfecting press Press capable of printing both sides of the paper during a single pass.

Also called 'duplex press' and 'perfector'.

perforations A line of small holes to ease tearing the paper at a specified place.

pH The pH value is a measure of the strength of the acidity or alkalinity of a paper. A pH of 0 is very acid, 14 is very alkaline, 7 is neutral.

photochromatic ink Ink that goes from clear to coloured when exposed to UV rays and sunlight, then back to clear when unexposed.

photographic proof Coloured proof made from film separations such as chromalin matchprint, Fuji Color Art, etc.

picking The release of surface fibres from paper during printing, resulting in small blank areas.

PIRA Printing Industries Research Association.

plate Paper, metal, plastic or rubber carrying an image to be reproduced on a printing press.

plate glazing Method of producing a smooth surface on sheets of generally handmade paper by placing them between polished plates of zinc or copper and passing the pack back and forth with slight friction between pressing rollers.

plate paper Paper designed for copperplate printing.

platesinking Debossing an area, on a page or cover, to hold a tipped-in picture or label.

ply A layer of paper or board, joined to others for strength. The resulting paper or board will be described as two-ply, three-ply, etc. depending on the number of layers.

pocket Envelope one side or centre seam, a bottom flap and opening on the shortside.

polypropylene A flexible plastic sheet available in many different colours, clear and frosted.

pop-up A term for collapsible three-dimensional structures and mechanics made from paper.

portrait Orientation in which height is greater than width.

PPA Periodical Publishers' Association.

Ppi Pages per inch – term used in US to specify paper thickness.

PPIC Pulp and Paper Information Centre.

presspahn Glazed board, which is extremely durable and moisture resistant. Originally produced for industrial applications, but useful for folders and covers.

press proofs In colour reproduction, a proof of a colour subject on a printing press, in advance of the production run.

printings Papers designed for letterpress printing.

progressive proofs Proofs made from the separate plates in colour-process work, showing the sequence of printing and the result after each additional colour has been applied; helps identify problems. Also called 'progs'.

proof Limited print run, taken from printing plates, usually on a flat-bed press, to enable the work to be checked before printing.

pulp Main ingredient in the papermaking process, usually made from processed wood, cotton linters or rags.

punch To cut shapes in paper or paperboard using a die. See **die-cut**

quarto A sheet of paper that is folded in half on the long side twice, to make a section of four leaves or eight pages.

quire 24 sheets of handmade paper, 25 sheets of machine-made paper, a twentieth part of a ream. See **volume/quantity of paper**

rag Cotton rag used as the principal raw material in the papermaking process. 'Rag content' describes the amount of cotton fibre relative to the total amount of material used in the pulp. The term is not widely used now, or is a misnomer, as more and more high-quality paper is made not from rag but from linters. See **cotton**

rattle The sound produced by shaking a piece of paper. In general, the harder the rattle, the better the quality, although there are exceptions.

170 **ream** A quantity of paper: 480 sheets of handmade, 500 sheets of machine made – equal to 20 quires. See **volume/quantity of paper**

recycled This is a vague term used to describe a wide variety of types of paper. Very few papers are made entirely from recycled fibres – usually a proportion of virgin fibres is added for strength, the proportion varying from paper to paper. The 'recycled' content of a paper may include any of the following:
– pulp left over from the previous batch of papermaking
– pulp made from clean off cuts from virgin sheets, known as 'broke'
– pulp made from paper that has been printed on and used, then collected, sorted and re-pulped. It is often assumed that this sort of 'post-consumer waste' is the basic ingredient of all recycled papers, whereas some recycled papers, especially those that look very 'clean', have a very low post-consumer waste content.
The environmental reasons for using recycled paper include the following:
– it uses half the energy and one third of the water of virgin paper
– fewer chemicals are used, resulting in less effluent
– paper and board form about a half of all domestic waste; disposing of our waste is becoming increasingly expensive and difficult. See **environmentally friendly**

reel A length of paper wound on a core irrespective of diameter, width or weight. See **web**

register To position printing properly with regard to the edges of the paper and other printing on the same sheet so that all elements are 'in register'.

relief printing Method in which the inked areas are higher than the non-inked areas. Types of relief printing include: block printing, flexography and letter press.

repro paper Paper with a hard-sized coating and good absorbency character.

resilience Property of paper that allows it to return to normal after distortion.

retree Paper with small imperfections at reduced price.

reverse Type, graphic or illustration produced by printing ink around its outline, allowing the underlying colour or paper to show through and form the image.

ribbed Paper finish traditionally used for heavyweight Manilla papers.

rice paper A common misnomer applied to Asian papers, as rice rarely plays a part in the manufacture of papers in Asia.

roll Coating applied by rollers, usually on machine.

rough Term used to describe the surface texture of a sheet of handmade or mould-made paper when it is left to dry naturally.

rub Can occur on matt-coated paper when the peaks on the surface literally get rubbed off or act as an abrasive and remove the print surface from an adjacent sheet.

satin papers Papers that fall between matt- and gloss-coated papers and have some of the advantages of both. See **silk papers**

SC Abbreviation of supercalendered. See **calendered**

score To compress a straight line into the paper so that it folds more easily and accurately. Also called 'creasing'.

section Folded signature. See **bookbinding terms** *folio* and *signature*

security paper Paper with features which make counterfeiting difficult. See **cheque papers**

self-adhesive paper Paper with a self-adhesive coating protected by laminate on one side and a good surface suitable for printing on the other.

set off Image from the wet side of the sheet marking the reverse side of the sheet above. Anti-set-off spray is commonly used to help prevent this.

sexto A sheet of paper folded with a z-fold to form a section of six leaves or 12 pages. See **z-fold**

sextodecimo A sheet of paper that is folded in half on the long side four times to make a section of 16 leaves or 32 pages.

shadow zone Thicker area in a sheet of paper formed either side of the ribs on a single faced mould by the water being drawn out and attracting more fibres.

sheet Refers to a sheet of papers. The term 'good sheet' refers to a sheet which prints well.

sheet-fed printing Printing onto flat sheets as opposed to web. Is generally considered to be of higher quality than web printing because of the greater control of register. See **web**

shives Specks in finished paper caused by impurities in the raw material. Also called 'sheaves'.

short grain Paper in which the grain is parallel to the shorter edge of the sheet. See **grain**

shoulder Top of the side flap on a wallet envelope. Important for factory inserting machines.

show through When the image printed on one side of the paper is evident on the reverse.

silk papers Papers that fall between matt- and gloss-coated papers and have some of the advantages of both, such as:
– medium opacity and bulk
– can give high-quality reproduction, with good definition of details
– text printed on these papers reads well due to the low reflectivity of the surface.

silkscreen printing Method of printing by using a squeegee to force ink through a meshed fabric screen. In addition to paper, it can be used to print a wide variety of materials which would not go through the rollers of a litho press, for example, card, plastic, fabric, metal. Good for bold designs, blocks of colour; less good for delicate work. Can be problematic for very light papers (can shrink after printing) and uncoated stocks (can take a long time to dry).

simulator paper A thin, translucent paper, more commonly known as tracing paper.

size Substance, originally glue or gelatine, used to reduce the rate at which paper absorbs water or ink. Can be incorporated in the pulp or applied to the finished sheet. See **engine sized** and **tub sized**

sizes of paper The ISO (International Organisation for Standardisation) series of paper measurements is the only system of measurement used in the machine-made paper trade, though its three denominations, 'A', 'B' and 'C', are not necessarily applicable to newspapers, books or some stationery items.
The 'A' series is used to denote paper sizes for general printing matter, 'B' is primarily for posters and wall charts and 'C' is specifically for envelopes. Dimensions in millimetres:
'A' series
AO *841 x 1,189* ***A1*** *594 x 841* ***A2*** *420 x 594* ***A3*** *297 x 420* ***A4*** *210 x 297* ***A5*** *148 x 210* ***A6*** *105 x 148* ***A7*** *74 x 105* ***A8*** *55 x 74* ***A9*** *37 x 55* ***A10*** *28 x 37* ***4AO*** *1,682 x 2,378* ***2AO*** *1,189 x 1,681*
'B' series
Trimmed sizes falling between A sizes designed for large items, for instance posters.
BO *1,000 x 1,414* ***B1*** *707 x 1,000* ***B2*** *500 x 707* ***B3*** *353 x 500* ***B4*** *250 x 353* ***B5*** *176 x 250* ***4B*** *2,000 x 2,828* ***2B*** *1,414 x 2,000*
'C' series
Envelopes and folders to take A series contents.
CO *917 x 1297* ***C1*** *648 x 917* ***C2*** *458 x 648* ***C3*** *324 x 458* ***C4*** *229 x 324* ***C5*** *162 x 229* ***C6*** *114 x 162* ***C7/6*** *81 x 162* ***C7*** *81 x 114* ***DL*** *110 x 220*
ISO series untrimmed stock sizes
The untrimmed paper sizes of the ISO 'A' series, which are intended to be trimmed to 'A' sizes after printing, are made in the following additional denominations, used mainly in machine-made paper designations. The 'RA' series (addition of an 'R' to the 'A' series) is for non-bled printing and includes approximately an extra 10–20mm onto the 'A' size which is trimmed off after printing. The 'SRA' series (addition of an 'SR' to the 'A' series) is used when printed work is bled off the edge of trimmed size and an extra 30–40mm is allowed on the 'A' size for trimming after printing is completed, for example, ***A2*** *420 x 594* ***RA2*** *430 x 610* ***SRA2*** *450 x 640*

Imperial sizes

Imperial measurements were used in Britain from 1836 until metrication. The picturesque names given to the sheet sizes were derived from the watermarks used by the old mills – different mills made different sizes of paper. Although machine-made paper is now sold in metric measurements, some of the more common Imperial terms, such as those listed below, are still referred to, especially for handmade paper.

crown 508 x 381 *double crown* 508 x 762 *quad crown* 762 x 1016
imperial 762 x 559 *half imperial* 381 x 559 *double imperial* 762 x 1118
foolscap 343 x 432 *double foolscap* 432 x 686 *quad foolscap* 686 x 864

The name foolscap derives from the fact that it used to have a watermark of a court jester's hat.

slot A die-cut in a piece of paper into which another piece of paper can be inserted.

smalts The finely powered cobalt blue glass used in loading. See **loading**

smoothness The smoothness of a paper is essentially the flatness of its surface. It is not the same as 'gloss', which is an optical property.

soy-based inks Inks using vegetable oils instead of petroleum products as pigments, which are more environmentally friendly.

spot colour Varnish or Ink applied only to a specific area rather than to the whole sheet.

spread Describes two adjacent pages when opened out flat. Also called 'double page spread'.

stock A term loosely applied to papermaking material in all its stages, but also refers to the wet pulp before it is fed on to the paper machine.

straw For environmental reasons, straw is being used as an alternative to wood fibre in papermaking, although not yet on a large scale.

string score Score created by pressing a string against the paper, as compared to scoring using a metal edge. See **score**

substance Weight of paper and board. See **gsm**

substrate Any substance or material on which printing is done.

supercalender Off-machine calender stack of alternate hard and soft rolls to impart smoothness and gloss. Also called 'sc'. See **calender**

surface finish The surface character of a sheet of paper, for instance, CP, HP, Not, burnished, hammered, etc.

surface sized Process in which paper is soaked in size following manufacture. Also called 'tub sized'. See **size** and **engine sized**

synthetic papers Papers made from synthetic material rather than natural, such as Tyvek®.

tab A small strip or piece of material attached to, or projecting from, something, used to hold, fasten, or manipulate it, or for identification and information.

TCF (Totally Chlorine-Free) TCF pulps are made without any chlorine compounds.

texture Surface of the sheet. Can be a natural result of pulp and processing or a contrived impression applied to the surface.

thermochromatic ink Ink that changes colour, appears or disappears as temperature alters.

thermography Technique of applying powder resin onto wet ink to produce a raised, glossy surface after heating. Used for logos on letterheads – effect is like die stamping, but cheaper.

thermo-mechanical pulp Made by heating chips of wood under pressure.

thickness of paper See **calliper**

throat Gap between the scoreline and back flap of a wallet envelope. A critical design aspect for most inserting machines.

thumb cut Shape cut from a pocket, wallet or book to facilitate access to contents.

ticket board A name for pasteboard, although coated board can be included in this grade.

tissue paper Very thin, lightweight paper for interleaving and wrapping.

tooth Characteristic, rough texture of a paper surface.

top side Opposite of wire side, the side of paper away from the wire during manufacture.

tracking Relative positions of pages that are inked in the cylinder rotation direction and follow one behind the other. Therefore images in the same track cannot be treated separately in terms of ink feed.

trap To print one ink over another or to print a coating, such as varnish, over an ink. The second liquid traps the first liquid.

trim Area surrounding the page or image area.

trimmed size Size of paper once trimmed.

triplex board Board made from three layers or lined on both sides.

twin wire Papers and boards made from two separate webs on a twin-wire paper machine.

two sidedness Term given to paper or board that exhibits different surface characteristics on either side of the sheet.

Tyvek® Made by Dupont from high-density polyethylene fibres, it has a very high strength, is lightweight and can be printed on in the same way as paper. Widely used for envelopes.

um Abbreviation of micron, 1/1000mm, used to measure the thickness of a sheet of paper.

uncoated mechanical sc A smooth, supercalendered stock providing good halftone reproduction. A lightweight, cheap alternative to coated paper.

uncoated papers See **matt-uncoated papers**

UV varnish Matt or gloss protective coating which is hardened using ultra-violet light. Can be prone to cracking along the spine.

varnish Liquid applied as a coating for protection and appearance, can be matt or gloss.

vellum Paper made from the inner side of calfskin. The term is also used to describe papers made from other materials that imitate real vellum.

vellum finish A toothy finish, which is relatively absorbent for fast ink penetration.

velvet papers See **silk papers**

virgin paper Paper made from virgin fibre (fibre used for the first time).

volume Thickness of paper expressed as volume for book production.

volume/quantity of paper
– Ream: 480 sheets of handmade, 500 sheets of machine made
– Quire: 24 sheets of handmade, 25 sheets of machine made
– Millpack: 100–125 sheets

wallet Envelope style with two side seams and the opening on the long edge.

waste Unusable paper or paper damage during normal make-ready, printing or binding operations, as compared to spoilage.

watermark A translucent design in a sheet of paper that can be seen when it is held up to the light. Watermarks are made by incorporating a raised device into the mould when the paper is made so that part of the paper is thinner and therefore translucent. Most watermarks are linear designs, but some – *chiaroscuro* watermarks – are made by putting a sculptured device into the mould to produce results such as the Queen's head found on British bank notes. Watermarks are generally read from the right side of the paper.

web The reel of wound paper in its entire width at the end of a paper machine prior to splitting into smaller rolls or cutting into sheets. Also called 'mother roll'.

web offset A form of offset litho, this process prints and sometimes finishes in one continuous pass onto a web of paper. When heat is used to facilitate finishing it is called 'heat set'. This can lead to the subsequent expansions of pages when atmospheric moisture is absorbed. When combined with sheet-fed covers the web-text pages often protrude after trimming. It is generally used for high-volume work such as magazines and, though it is poorly perceived, dramatic improvements in quality have been made in recent years.

172

weight Weight or grammage of a sheet of paper, normally expressed in gsm.

window Aperture in envelope usually covered with glassine paper. Also refers to a die-cut hole in a printed product that reveals an image on the sheet behind it.

wire part In papermaking, the moving belt of woven phosphor bronze or nylon on which the pulp falls to make the paper web, and which thus determines the grain direction of the fibres.

wireside The surface of the pulp that is in contact with the mesh during papermaking. Also called 'wiremark'.

wood free Papers which are made of chemically pulped wood (as opposed to mechanically pulped) are sometimes referred to as 'wood-free' papers. Also called 'free sheet'.

wood pulp Wood pulp is made by chemically or mechanically processing wood. The majority of papers are now made from wood pulp rather than, for instance, cotton/rag pulp.

work and tumble To print one side of a sheet of paper, then turn the sheet over from gripper to back using the same side guide and plate to print the second side.

work and turn To print one side of a sheet of paper, then turn the sheet over from left to right and print the second side using the same plate. The same gripper and lay edge are used for printing both sides.

wove papers Papers made in wove moulds, as opposed to laid moulds. In a wove mould the covering screen is made of woven wire, similar to the warp and weft in cloth, and the resulting paper has no obvious markings.

xerographic paper Paper made to reproduce well in copy machines and laser printers.

xuan The Chinese word for paper.

z-fold A way of creating a 12- or 24-page section in a book. A sheet of paper is first folded in thirds against the grain – the z-fold. Folding this in half with the grain gives a six-leave section – a sexto. Folding the sexto in half with the grain gives a 12-leave section – a duodecimo.

zipper A device that allows sealed packages/envelopes to be easily opened. Comprises of two parallel lines of die-cut slots, cleverly angled to control the tear of the paper or card.

The author would like to thank the following for their help and contribution:
Rebekah Doody
Bruno Jones
John Stone

Photographic credits
P17 Richard Learoyd, p29 Jimmy Fok, p58 Gueorgui Pinkhassov (Magnum Photos), p63 Duncan Smith, p71 Kevin Summers, p74 Jimmy Fok and Peter Merlin, p76 Tom Schierlitz, p91 Jimmy Fok and Peter Merlin, p103-7 Hiroyuki Hirai, p108 Richard Davies, p114 Andreas von Einsiedel, p120 Anders Sune Berg (courtesy of Gallery Koch and Kesslau, Berlin), p123 Kazumi Kurigami, p128 David Scheinmann, p132 Sarah Jones, p144 Mikiya Takimoto, Koichi Kuroda and Kazuki Suzuki.

Reading list
D. A. Carter and J. Diaz, *The Elements of Pop-Up* (Simon & Schuster Children's Books, New York, 1999)
R. Fawcett-Tang, C. Foges and J. O'Reilly, *Experiment Formats* (RotoVision, East Sussex, 2001)
A. Fuad-Luke, *The Eco-Design Handbook* (Thames & Hudson, London, 1999)
W. Harvey, *The Best of Brochure Design 07* (Rockport, Massachusetts, 2003)
M. McQuaid, *Shigeru Ban* (Phaidon Press, London, 2003)
Keith A. Smith, *Smith's Sewing Single Sheets – Non-Adhesive Binding*, volume IV (Keith Smith Books, New York, 2001)
N. Williams, *Paperwork* (Phaidon Press, London, 1993)
Hand Papermaking, volume 19, number 1, summer 2004
How to Fold (The Pepin Press, Agile Rabbit Editions, New York, 2002)

Websites
American Forest and Paper Association – www.afandpa.org
Confederation of European Paper Industries – www.cepi.org
Paper Profile, voluntary environmental product declaration guide – www.paperprofile.com
Memorandum by the Paper Federation of Great Britain – www.publications.parliament.uk/pa/cm199900/cmselect/cmenvtra/903/903m52.htm
US Enviromental Protection Agency – www.epa.gov
EPA report on 'Municipal Solid Waste, Paper and Paperboard' – www.epa.gov/epaoswer/non-hw/muncpl/paper.htm
Articles on Japan Pavilion, EXPO 2000, Hannover – www.designboom.com/history/ban_expo.html
www.takenaka.co.jp/takenaka_e/t-file_e/hannover_e
Cardboard Building, Westborough Primary Shool – www.cardboardschool.co.uk
British Association of Paper Historians – www.baph.org.uk
Glossary of bookbinding terms – www.redmark.co.nz/gla-e.htm
Glossary of Printing and Graphic terms – www.printindustry.com/glossary.htm
History of Japanese paper and paper names – www.cedarseed.com/journeys/jappaper.html
www.swicofil.com/products/060paperyarn.html

Aare, **111**
accessories, **95, 130–2**
acetate, **63**
Agle, **144**
Agripina, **79, 85**
Allingham Hansen, **149**
alternative materials
    aluminium, **87, 105, 155**
    Astro Turf, **91**
    canvas, **130**
    glass, **158**
    plastics/PVC, **52, 63, 86,
    102, 153**
    polyester, **132**
    polypropylene, **86, 169**
    steel/stainless steel, **86,
    105, 158**
    Skivertex Vicuana, **23**
    tin, **117**
    'Touch'-style rubber, **89**
    Tyvek®, **124, 128, 157, 171**
    wood, **105, 155**
Altura Gloss, **58**
Andrew Vaccari, **147**
annual reports, **21, 56, 74, 79,
    85, 91**
Araveal, **38**
architecture, **94, 99–108**
art paper and board, **20, 29,
    58, 74, 88, 91, 161**
    gloss-coated art paper,
    67, 76, 166
    matt-coated art paper, **16,
    21, 22, 23, 38, 45, 49, 58,
    65, 67, 68, 79, 85, 88, 90,
    144, 168**
    satin-coated art paper, **37,
    111, 144, 170**
    silk-coated art paper, **48, 49,
    58, 62, 83, 86, 88, 170**
Artecnica, **157**
Artomatic, **67**
Astralux Label, **25**
Atelier Works, **16, 78**
Austin, Paul, **25, 48**
Australia, **58**
Avery Sass Laminate, **71**
Avison, Tracy, **62**

badges, **131**
bags, **52, 130, 136, 142, 150**

baking parchment, **85**
Ban, Shigeru, **94,
    102–8, 152–3**
Bartels, Yke, **88**
Beauregard Printers, **19**
Belgium, **114**
Benson, Paula, **86**
Bertholle, Marie, **57, 67**
bible paper, **16, 17, 65, 72,
    73, 161**
Bierut, Michael, **27**
Billes, **73**
binding, **12, 53–68, 161**
    bookbinding terms, **162–3**
    cloth binding, **55, 65, 67, 68,
    83, 85**
    rubber/elastic bands, **60,
    61, 62**
    Singer sewn binding, **63,
    83, 163**
    Swiss binding, **65, 163**
    wiro binding, **12, 56, 57**
Biotop two-sided satin, **37**
BLM Trade Printers, **19, 48**
bond paper, **47, 56, 138, 163**
books, **16, 28, 35, 43, 59,
    68, 90**
    annuals, **22**
    commemorative, **27, 42,
    63, 88**
    flick books, **62, 78**
    interactive, **88**
    notebooks, **60**
    sample books, **55**
    in sculpture, **116–7**
Boontje, Tord, **157**
Borchgrave, Isabelle de, **114**
Boss Print, **21, 37, 41, 50**
boxes, **44–5, 113, 138–41,
    143, 150**
Boy Meets Girl S&J, **61**
Brazil, **155**
brochures, **25, 30, 48, 58**
Brown, Rita, **114**
Bruketa, Davor, **79, 85**
Bruketa & Zinic, **79, 85**
Buro Happold, **101, 107, 108**

calendars, **38, 66**
Callesen, Peter, **120**
Campana, Fernando and

Humberto, **155**
Campana Objetos, **155**
Canada, **19, 48, 114**
candle holders, **149**
Canson Ingre, **138**
Capital Box, **48**
Cappellini, **152**
card, **157**
    art card, **20, 43, 74**
    corrugated, **141, 164**
    gloss-coated card, **58**
    matt-coated card, **88**
    matt-uncoated card, **46,
    57, 168**
    playing cards, **37**
    satin-coated card, **40, 170**
card and board, **157**
    foil laminated, **62**
    gloss-coated, **59**
    Altura, **58**
    greyboard, **32, 56, 64, 111,
    149, 166**
    matt-coated, **38**
    Ensocoat, **88**
    metallic, **62**
    Stardream Silver
    two-sided, **62**
    pearlized, **113**
    satin-coated Biotop
    two-sided, **37**
cardboard, **88, 101, 148**
cardboard tubes, **76, 94,
    152, 164**
cards
    business cards, **19, 25, 37,
    40, 44, 86**
    greetings cards, **18, 40, 46,
    73, 80**
Carmody, Sean, **42**
Carter Wong Tomlin, **50, 136**
Cartlidge, Ian, **17**
Cartlidge Levene, **17, 58**
cartridge paper, **40, 44, 47
    127, 164**
Casparie, **64**
cast-coated paper, **67, 76, 144,
    164, 166**
catalogues, **32, 52, 57,
    61, 64–5**
CD covers and packaging,
    76, 144

173

174

Centaure, **135**
chairs, **96, 152, 160**
Chalayan, Hussein, **95, 124**
Challenger Offset, **50**
Chantani, Masahiro, **47, 94**
Chappell, Andrea, **76**
chipboard, **80, 164**
Chromalux, **25**
Clark, Nick, **89**
clocks, **148**
clothing, **95, 114, 123–8**
coat hangers, **149**
Coley, Laura, **138**
Colorado, **88**
Colorplan, **25, 37, 55**
Colortec, **57**
Colour Graphics, **148**
Colourscan, **74, 91**
Command matt, **21**
Comme des Garçons
  Noir, **123**
Consort Royal Brilliance, **48**
Consorti, Carol Pierre, **43**
Consorti Royal Silk, **86**
Cooley, Helen, **62, 83**
copy paper, **35, 120, 164**
corrugated board, **114, 148,
  150, 154, 155, 164**
Cottrell and Vermeulen, **94, 101**
Courier Super Wove, **86**
cover paper and board,
  113, 165
covers
  annual reports, **21**
  books, **16, 27, 42, 43, 55, 68**
  brochures, **25**
  catalogues, **32, 52, 57**
  CDs, **76**
  debossed, **23, 83**
  diaries, **23**
  embossed, **25, 64, 65, 87, 89**
  laminated, **55**
  lenticular, **90, 168**
  magazines, **36**
Coyne, Anthony, **23**
craft paper, **148, 155**
Crawford, Kath, **62, 83, 89**
crêpe paper, **127, 165**
Croatia, **79, 85, 154**
CTD Capita, **62**
CTD Printers, **17**

cutting, **12, 35–40, 42–3**
  kirigami, **94, 167**
  kiss-cutting, **71, 168**
  laser-cutting, **12, 42–3, 47,
    142, 168**
  perforations, **35, 79, 85, 169**
  see also die-cutting

Davies, Justin, **23**
Davies, Nigel, **89**
Dehning, Heike, **88**
Denmark, **120**
Design East, **86**
diaries, **23**
die-cutting, **12, 165**
  in books and magazines, **23,
    35, 36**
  in brochures and reports,
    38, 79
  in furniture, **154**
  in greetings cards, **40, 46**
  in packaging, **76, 135, 138**
  in posters, **48**
  in stationery, **19, 37, 40**
DKP Finishing, **50**
Draft, **18, 38, 46, 60, 66,
  80, 140**
Draught Associates, **148**
Dreßen, Markus, **36**
Drukkerij Aeroprint, **32, 37, 59**
Drukkerij Koenders & Van
  Steijn, **88**
Drukkerij Plantijn, **64**
Dufex, **27, 165**
duplex papers and boards,
  55, 165
Durrant, Nathan, **40**
Dye, Alan, **27, 50, 56, 72, 73**

E flute board craft, **148, 164**
Eagleton, Nick, **89**
Eatock, Daniel, **61**
Edmondson, Bryan, **55, 65**
egg boxes, **15**
Elixir Design, **40**
Ellul, Jamie, **41**
Empress Litho, **63**
Ensocoat, **88**
envelopes, **18, 19, 56, 124,
  131, 172**
Enveloppe Laurentide, **19**

EricandMarie, **57, 67**
Ernstberger, Matthias, **30, 47**
Essex Tube Windings, **101**
Eurobulk, **88**
Ex-Libris, UK, **67**
exhibition pieces, **94, 113–14,
  117, 119**

Fabio Ongarato Design, **58**
Fabriano Spa, **127**
Farmer, Jennie, **116**
fashion items, **95, 114, 121–32**
Felton, **46, 80**
Fernedge, **45, 138**
Finney, Nick, **27, 50, 56, 72, 73**
Fiorini International, Italy, **136**
Fluesand, **60**
fluorescent paper, **28**
foil papers and boards, **62, 166**
  Dufex, **27, 165**
  foil laminates, **27**
  holographic foil, **75**
  silver foil, **85**
Folders Galore, **89**
folding, **12, 41, 44–5, 48, 50–2,
  57, 58, 138**
  concertina folds, **12, 50, 164**
  French folds, **12, 85, 90, 162**
  interactive examples, **34, 98,
    110, 146**
  origami, **12, 72, 73, 94, 101,
    116, 143, 167**
  see also cutting
Foley, Greg, **43**
Form, **86**
'43 dreams,' **43**
Fox River Coronado, **119**
Fox River Crushed leaf, **119**
France, **57, 67**
Franklin, CG, **101**
Freedman, Joe, **47**
Frei, Otto, **107**
Fuchs, Julia, **30**
Fulmar Colour, **58**
furniture, **96, 152–5**

Ga Bagasse soft, **140**
Galerie Art Silk, **83**
Gaspar, Éric, **57, 67**
Gavin Martin Associates, **15,
  25, 83, 87**

Gehry, Frank O, **96**
Gengo Matsui, **102**
Germany, **36, 158**
GF Smith Biblio, **65**
Gilbert Esse Texture, **19**
Gilbert Gilclear Oxford, **19**
Giles, Adam, **50**
Glad Filter Face, **71**
glassine, **18, 166**
gloss-coated art, **76**
Goddard, Cherry, **76**
Good News Press, **86**
Goodwin, Frankie, **52**
Graphic Metal Company, **87**
Graphic Thought Facility,
  49, 150
greaseproof paper, **143, 166**
Greece, **99**
greyboard, **32, 56, 64, 111,
  149, 166**
Gumuchdjian, Philip, **94, 108**

handmade paper, **8, 128, 166**
HannoArt Silk, **48**
Happy Forsman & Bodenfors,
  73, 111
Hard, Nick, **86**
Hasting, Julia, **68**
hat-trick design, **15, 21, 25, 37,
  41, 50**
Hawkins, David, **16**
Helflin, Mark, **22**
Hello Gloss, **88**
Hello Silk, **88**
Hepadru, **88**
Hestia House, **47**
HGV Design, **75**
high-gloss art, **67, 76, 166**
Hiscock, Clifford, **23**
Holmquist, Holly, **40**
honeycomb board, **101, 105,
  108, 166**
honeycomb tissue paper, **160**
Hong Kong Graphics and
  Printing, **49**
Hoshino, Shuichi, **102**
Howard, Glenn, **78**
Howat, Gareth, **15, 21, 25, 37,
  41, 50**

IBL, **79, 85**
Impressions, **50**
information packs, **38**
interactive design, **12, 69–80,
  88, 124**
invitations, **15, 17, 20, 27, 47,
  48, 50, 55**
Iridium, **19**
Italy, **143**
Ito, Kei, **128–9, 132**

Jackson, Chris, **148**
Jae Kim Printing Company, **30**
Japan
  architecture, **102–7**
  business cards, **44**
  calendars, **38, 66**
  fashion items, **123**
  furniture, **152, 160**
  greetings cards, **18, 40,
    46, 80**
  information packs, **38**
Japanese Pavilion, Hanover
  Expo, **93, 107**
Kobe housing project, **102–3**
  lights, **158**
Museum for Children's
  Art, **105**
  notebooks, **60**
  packaging, **140–1, 144**
  promotional material, **113**
  window displays, **113**
Japanese paper, **7–8, 93, 95,
  123, 127, 144, 158, 167**
Japanese Pavilion, Hanover
  Expo, **93, 106–7**
Jerde, Jennifer, **40**
jewellery, **93, 95**
Jinnai, Akiko, **113**
Joh Enschedé Security Printing,
  Netherlands, **75**
johnson banks, **45, 71**
Jones, Ryan, **65**
Jones & Palmer, **56**

Kalape, **66**
Kaneko, Eiichiro, **102**
Karlsson, Hjalti, **22, 76**
Kawakubo, Rei, **123**
Ken Miki & Associates, **38, 40,
  44, 46**

Kessels, Erik, **32, 64**
KesselsKramer, **32, 37, 59, 64**
Kestrel Offset, **48**
Kimpton, David, **15, 21, 25, 37,
  41, 50**
Kinetic Singapore, **20, 29,
  74, 91**
Kinko Package Company, **140**
Kiock, Valerie, **23**
Kitchen, The, **67**
Kittel, Andreas, **73**
Klimpel, Oliver, **36**
Kobe housing project, **102–3**
Koehn, Maria, **36**
Koeweiden-postma, **37**
Koford Press, **29**
Kolegram, **48**
Konig, Anne, **36**
Kornestedt, Anders, **111**
Krista, Rozema, **32**
Ksenija Jurenic, **154**
Kudos, Johnschen, **90**
Kysen, **135**

lamination, **55, 94, 111, 168**
Lava, **88**
Le Scott, **86**
L'Écuyer, Mario, **19**
lense tissue paper, **114, 168**
Lessebo Linné, **73**
letterheads, **19, 25, 37, 86**
lights, **96, 153, 155–9**
Lim, Lin, **20**
Lim, Pann, **20, 29, 74, 91**
linen paper, **128, 168**
Lippa Pearce Design, **15**
Lok, Andrew, **20**
Louwé, Harmine, **64**
Lyon, Marcus, **87**

machine-coated paper and
  board, **32, 37, 168**
MacMillan, Hazel, **138**
MadeThought, **25, 48**
magazines, **27, 36**
mailers, **45, 50, 87**
'MaMo Nouchies' lights, **158**
manuals, **89**
Match, **42**

matt-coated art paper, **16, 21, 22, 23, 32, 38, 45, 49, 58, 65, 67, 68, 79, 85, 88, 90, 144, 168**
matt-coated board, **36, 37, 42**
matt-uncoated art paper, **25, 27, 37, 38, 47, 50, 52, 55, 57, 63, 65, 78, 80, 86, 88, 119, 168**
Maurer, Ingo, **158**
McConnell, John, **138**
Mennonites, The, **16**
menus, **50**
Miki, Ken, **38, 40, 44, 46**
Millennium Real Art, **58**
Miller, Abbott, **90, 119**
Milt Ga, **140**
MIT, **79, 85**
Mivan, **108**
mixed media, **12, 81–91**
Mizoguchi, Sachiko, **143**
M&M Bell, **138**
models, **45, 73, 94, 99–100**
Moderatone, **18**
Mohawk Superfine, **27**
Mombach, Dagmar, **158**
Moore, **55, 65**
Muir, Sam, **67**
Museum for Children's Art, Japan, **104–5**

Nakajima, Hideki, **144**
Nakajima Design, **144**
Naturalis, **65**
NB: Studio, **27, 50, 56, 72, 73**
Neale, Paul, **49**
Neptune, **63**
Neptune Unique, **58**
Netherlands
  architectural models, **99**
  books, **59, 88**
  catalogues, **32, 64**
  letterheads, **37**
  products, **150**
New V matt, **38**
Newark, Quentin, **16, 78**
newsprint, **30, 36, 101, 124, 169**
Noguchi, Isamu, **96, 158**
Northwards, **148**

Oblitas, Ramiro, **73**
Offenbach bible paper, **17**
Ogawa, Naoki, **38**
OK Bright Rough, **38**
Ongarato, Fabio, **58**
Oxford, **19**

packaging, **95, 133–44, 148, 153**
Paper Marc, **101**
paper quality, **7–8, 12, 13–32**
  opacity, **19, 169**
  transparency, **18, 19, 66**
  see also surface effects
paper stocks
  Agripina, **79, 85**
  Araveal, **38**
  art, **29**
  Astralux Label, **25**
  Avery Sass Laminate, **71**
  baking parchment, **85**
  bible, **16, 17, 65, 72, 73, 161**
  bond, **47, 56, 138, 163**
  Canson Ingre, **138**
  cartridge, **40, 44, 47, 127, 164**
  cast-coated, **67, 76, 144, 164, 166**
  Centaure, **135**
  Challenger Offset, **50**
  Chromalux, **25**
  Colorado, **88**
  Colorplan, **25, 37, 55**
  Command matt, **21**
  Consort Royal Brilliance, **48**
  Consorti Royal Silk, **86**
  copy, **35, 120, 164**
  Courier Super Wove, **86**
  craft, **148, 155**
  crêpe, **127, 165**
  Dufex, **27, 165**
  Ensocoat, **88**
  Eurobulk, **88**
  Fabriano Spa, **127**
  Felton, **46, 80**
  flame-resistant, **107**
  Fluesand, **60**
  fluorescent, **28**
  Fox River Coronado, **119**
  Fox River Crushed Leaf, **119**
  Ga Bagasse soft, **140**

Galerie Art Silk, **83**
GF Smith Biblio, **65**
Gilbert Esse Texture, **19**
Gilbert Gilclear Oxford, **19**
Glad Filter Face, **71**
glassine, **18, 166**
gloss-coated art, **67, 76, 166**
greaseproof, **143, 166**
handmade, **8, 128, 166**
HannoArt Silk, **48**
Hello, **88**
Japanese, **7–8, 93, 95, 123, 127, 144, 158, 167**
Kalape, **66**
Kestrel Offset, **48**
lense tissue, **114, 168**
Lessebo Linné, **73**
linen, **128, 168**
machine-coated, **32**
matt-coated art, **16, 22, 32, 36–8, 42, 45, 49, 67, 68, 144, 168**
matt-uncoated art, **25, 27, 37, 38, 47, 50, 52, 55, 57, 63, 65, 78, 80, 86, 88, 119, 168**
Millenium Real Art, **58**
Milt Ga, **140**
Moderatone, **18**
Mohawk Superfine, **27**
Naturalis, **65**
Neptune, **63**
Neptune Unique, **58**
New V matt, **38**
newsprint, **30, 36, 101, 124, 169**
Offenbach, **17**
OK Bright Rough, **38**
Paperback, **15**
Parilux 1S, **58**
Parilux Silk, **62**
pattern-making, **114**
pearlized, **113**
Phoenix Motion, **52**
PhoeniXmotion Xenon, **78**
Premier Essential Gloss, **23**
Premier Essential Offset, **23**
Premier Naturalis, **50**
recycled, **8–9, 15, 19, 35, 88, 93, 96, 119, 170**
Reporle, **80**

Reviva, **88**
satin-coated art, **37, 111, 144, 170**
self-adhesive, **71, 170**
silk-coated art, **48, 49, 58, 62, 83, 86, 88, 170**
Skye Brilliant White, **50**
stencil, **123**
Strathmore Writing, **47**
sugar, **15**
Take-bulky, **18**
Tullis stamp, **75**
uncoated, **25, 27, 37, 38, 47, 50, 52, 55, 61, 63, 65, 78, 80, 86, 88, 119, 144, 168**
waterproofed, **94, 107, 155**
wood-free, **49, 64, 74, 91, 172**
Xenon, **90**
Yselprint, **59**
Yupo, **113**
Zanders Zeta Smooth, **41**
paper tubes, **94, 101–8, 152–3**
Paperback, **15**
papier mâché, **93, 96, 147, 169**
Parilux 1S gloss, **58**
Parilux Silk, **62**
Parker, Ben, **25, 48**
Partners, The, **62, 83, 87, 89, 142**
Pastel Company, **140**
pattern-making paper, **114**
Patterson, Simon, **101**
Pawson, Mark, **28, 35, 131**
Pearce, Harry, **15**
pearlized cover paper, **113**
Pentagram, London, **138**
Pentagram, New York, **27, 42, 90, 119**
Perivan Creative Print, **48, 52**
pet houses, **93, 147**
Petrie, Rob, **67**
Phaidon Press, **16, 68**
Phoenix Motion, **52**
PhoeniXmotion Xenon, **78**
Photofabrication, **86**
picture frames, **74, 111**
Pietsch, Stefan, **58**
pin board, **101**

PJ Print, **61**
Poh, Roy, **20, 29, 74, 91**
pop-ups, **12, 46, 169**
posters, **28, 48, 73**
pre-manufactured egg boxes, **15**
Premier Essential Gloss, **23**
Premier Essential Offset, **23**
Premier Naturalis, **50**
Principle Colour, **73**
products, **96, 145–60**
promotional material
  binding techniques, **58, 62, 67, 68**
  cutting techniques, **37, 42**
  exhibition pieces, **113**
  interactive design, **78**
  invitations, **15**
  mixed media, **83**

Quinton, Greg, **83, 87, 142**
Quinton and Kaines, **101**

Radford Wallis, **63**
Ramshaw, Wendy, **95**
Ratchford Windsor Craft, **83**
rebecca and mike, **124**
recycled paper, **8–9, 15, 19, 35, 88, 93, 96, 119, 170**
  in accessories, **130–1**
  in architecture, **101–8**
  books, **116**
  cardboard, **101**
  envelopes, **131**
  in furniture, **152, 154**
  in lights, **155**
  magazines, **130**
  maps, **131**
  mineral water labels, **117**
  newsprint, **101, 147**
  in packaging, **136**
  paper cups, **157**
  in paper tubes, **101, 102, 107, 108**
  posters, **150**
  in sculpture, **116–17, 124**
  see also papier mâché
Renwick, Jack, **83, 142**
Reporle, **80**
Reviva, **88**
Rice (George) & Sons, **27**

Robbins, Stewart, **153**
Roberts, Jamie, **55**
Robertson, Dana, **87**
Rozema, Krista, **56**

Sagmeister, Stefan, **22, 30, 47, 76**
Sagmeister Inc, **22, 30, 47, 76**
Sakaida, Shigeyuki, **38**
Sample, **68**
Sannichi Printing Company, **46, 80**
Sarabande Press, **47**
SAS, **52, 76**
satin-coated art paper, **37, 111, 144, 170**
Sayuri Studio, **113, 141**
Scher, Paula, **42**
sculpture, **94, 96, 116–17, 120**
SEA, **55, 65**
self-adhesive paper, **71, 170**
'Shared Ground,' Millennium Dome, **94, 108**
Shigeru Ban Architects, **102–7, 152–3**
Shimizu, Yoshiko, **141**
Shoji, Sayuri, **113, 141**
Shotech Press, **20**
silk-coated art paper, **48, 49, 58, 62, 83, 86, 88, 170**
Simpson, John, **55, 65**
Singapore, **20, 29, 74, 91**
68 Frank, **15**
Skivertex Vicuana, **23**
Sky Sora, Norika, **144**
Skye Brilliant White, **50**
Sleight, Rachael, **124–7**
slip cases, **16, 17, 37, 43, 119**
Smart, Gavin, **111**
Soh, Leng, **74, 91**
Sonoco Europe, **107, 108**
Spector cut + paste, **36**
Spence Associates, **94, 108**
St Joseph Corporation, **48**
Stafford, Paul, **148**
Stallinga, Henk, **88**
stamps, **71, 75**
Stardream Silver two-sided, **62**
stationery, **19, 25, 37, 41, 86, 138**
Ste Croix, Tony de, **87**

176

Steidl, **90**
stencil paper, **123**
Stott, Ben, **27, 50, 56, 72, 73**
Strathmore Writing paper, **47**
structural board, **101**
Studiomama, **148–9**
Studley Press, **119**
sugar paper, **15**
surface effects, **12, 13–32**
 blind debossing, **23, 25, 83, 165**
 blind embossing, **64, 138, 162**
 crumpling, **28–9, 73**
 embossing, **25, 27, 44, 65, 75, 87, 89, 165**
 foil-blocking, **25, 27, 83, 166**
 silkscreen printing, **15, 55, 86, 170**
 see also paper quality
Sutherland, Jim, **15, 21, 25, 37, 41, 50**
Sweden, **73, 111**
Switzerland, **117, 130, 155**

Taiyo Printing Company, **18, 38, 60, 66**
Take-bulky, **18**
Takenaka Europe, **107**
Taylor Bloxham, **23**
technical board, **74**
Teixeira, Mike, **48**
test brown, **148**
Tezuka, Minoru, **102**
Thaw, Jacqueline, **27**
Thomas, Gillian, **89**
three-dimensional design, **29, 44–5, 46, 93–160**
tissue paper, **67, 114, 160, 171**
Tokujin Yoshioka Design, **160**
Tolstrup, Nina, **149**
Tomlin, Matt, **52**
Towell, Larry, **16**
Trachsel, Sonja, **117, 130**
translucent paper, **8, 19, 67**
TSP Taiyo, **102**
TTB, **78**
Tullis Stamp Paper, **75**
two-dimensional design, **11–91**
2pm Limited, **148, 153**
Tyvek®, **124, 128, 157, 171**

Uchida, Mihoko, **102**
Uehara, Ryosuke, **38, 60, 80**
UK
 accessories, **131–2**
 annual reports, **21, 56**
 architecture, **101, 108**
 books, **16, 27, 28, 35, 55, 63**
 brochures, **25, 48, 58**
 catalogues, **52, 61, 65**
 diaries, **23**
 fashion items, **124–8**
 greetings cards, **73**
 invitations, **15, 17, 27, 50, 55**
 lights, **157**
 mailers, **45, 50, 87**
 manuals, **89**
 menus, **50**
 Millennium Dome project, **94, 108**
 packaging, **135–8, 142**
 posters, **48**
 products, **147–9, 150, 153**
 promotional material, **15, 37, 58, 62, 67, 78, 83**
 sculpture, **116**
 stamps, **71, 75**
 stationery, **25, 41, 86**
 Westborough Primary School, Essex, **94, 101**
uncoated paper, **25, 27, 37, 38, 47, 50, 52, 55, 61, 63, 65, 78, 80, 86, 88, 119, 144, 168**
Union Druckerei, **36**
USA
 books, **22, 42–3, 68, 90**
 brochures, **30**
 business cards, **40**
 CD covers, **76**
 exhibition pieces, **119**
 fashion items, **124**
 invitations, **47**
 magazines, **27**
 promotional material, **42**
UV varnish, **21, 36, 171**

Vaccari, Andrew, **147**
van der Muelen, Jos, **150**
Van Structural Design, **105**
Velbec Plastic, **52**

Ventura Press, **50**
Vincent, Nick, **27, 50**
Visionaire, **43**
Vyzoviti, Sophia, **99**

Wallis, Andrew, **63**
Walsall Security Printers, **71**
Wang, Miao, **47**
Warren, FJ, **27**
Wasser, Aoife, **43**
Watanabe, Yoshie, **18, 46, 66, 140**
waterproofed paper, **94, 107, 155**
Wendt, Gilmar, **52**
Wenzel, Jan, **36**
West, Paul, **86**
Westborough Primary School, Essex, **94, 101**
Westerham Press, **78**
Wettstein, Robert A, **155**
White Crescent acetate, **63**
Wightman, Jodie, **72**
williams and phoa, **23**
window displays, **94, 112–3**
Wolbers, Hans, **88**
wood-free paper, **49, 64, 74, 91, 172**

Xenon, **90**

Yoshioka, Tokujin, **160**
Young (R) & Son, **25**
Yselprint, **59**
Yupo, **113**

Zanders Zeta Smooth, **41**
'Zettel'z' lights, **158–9**
Zinic, Nikola, **79, 85**
Zwolsman, Hugo, **88**